# PARTY LIKE A CULINISTA

JILL DONENFELD + JOSETTH GORDON

*jill donenfeld + josetth gordon*

# PARTY LIKE A

# culinista ®

## FRESH RECIPES • BOLD FLAVORS • GOOD FRIENDS

LAKE ISLE PRESS, INC., NEW YORK

Published by:
Lake Isle Press, Inc.
2095 Broadway, Suite 301
New York, NY 10023
(212) 273-0796
E-mail: lakeisle@earthlink.net

Distributed to the trade by:
National Book Network, Inc.
4501 Forbes Boulevard, Suite 200
Lanham, MD 20706
1(800) 462-6420
www.nbnbooks.com

Library of Congress Control Number: 2011933325

ISBN-13: 978-1-891105-50-0

ISBN-10: 1-891105-50-7

Book and cover design: Ellen Swandiak

Editors: Stephanie White, Jennifer Sit

This book is available at special sales discounts for bulk purchases as premiums or special editions, including customized covers. For more information, contact the publisher at (212) 273-0796 or by e-mail, lakeisle@earthlink.net

First edition

Printed in the United States of America

10 9 8 7 6 5 4 3 2 1

THIS COOKBOOK IS DEDICATED TO OUR FAMILIES
WHO TAUGHT US TO COOK WITH LOVE,
SHARE THE TABLE, AND CELEBRATE.

# ACKNOWLEDGMENTS

Thanks to our taste-testers: Beryl Donenfeld, Jack Donenfeld, Barbara + Dick Allen, Diane + Carl Iseman, Nancy + Glenn Gollobin, Kim + Chris Neidtch, Leslie + Jim Fitzgerald, Leslie + Michael Krienes, Deborah + Randy Birckhead, Linda + Gary Greenberg, Celeste + John Warrington, Valerie + Rick Steinau, Barbara + Dick Allen, Ginger + Rob Rubin, Liz Stites, Ann Segal + Jerry Malsh, Sebastien Hue, Cassie + Brian Wissel, Lumen Sivitz, Eric Greenberg, Michelle Rothzeid, Alex Phillips, the Colonel Spice Man, Art the fish monger, Mr. Snyder, Arlene Brooks, Derrick Gordon, Mark Gordon, Sheraine Gordon, Shakean + Shakcon Crawford, Miles Milling, Ilan Folman-Cohen, Latoya Taylor, Ariana Getz, Matt Wilstein, and Maggie Piker.

Thanks to those who tested recipes for us: Ann Segal, Barbara Allen, Beryl Donenfeld, Charlotte Joseph, Deborah Birckhead, Fabia Ditcheff, Sandra Fluke, Ari + Ilan Folman-Cohen, Diane Iseman, Dollie Giddings, Hiroko Kiiffner, Jenn Sit, Kara Ohngren, Katie Han, Katie Houlbrook, Kim + Chris Neidtch, Leslie Kreines, Nancy Tuchman, Rainey Norins, Rebecca Oresman, Elaine Poon, Sam Kim, Sarah Chang, Stephanie White, Suzanne Kennedy, Taylor Thompson, Jane Frye, Kristy Zadrozny, Samantha Hilbert, and Valerie Steinau.

Thanks to Katie Han for helping to edit and for pitching in.

Thanks to Ben Liquet, Andrele Victor, Ariana Getz, Matt Wilstein, Jacob Moore, Marcy Roberts, and Jill's family for helping during the shoot.

Thank you to all the Culinistas from The Dish's Dish with such amazing skills in the kitchen. To Paloma Shutes, Jacob Moore, and Jane Frye for always being available to help out. To Chris Phillips, Gillian Schwartz, Eva Foust Yazhari, Samantha Hilbert Thomas, Tom Katis, Nick Bos, Nathaniel Schoen, and Richard Teichman for lots of support, generosity, and filling in the gaps. Thank you Gregory Goode for your talent as a photographer and for being a great friend. Thank you Meredith Fish, Tee, Allison Dalia, Craig, Phil Huang, and Keith Pepper for help setting up the shoot. Thank you Julie Taras, Tasha Garcia, Kate Betts, the Edens, Florence Fabricant, Rebecca Inocencio, and Richard Coraine.

Thanks to the team at Lake Isle Press: Hiroko Kiiffner, Stephanie White, and Jennifer Sit. Thanks also to our designer, Ellen Swandiak.

Thanks to Jesse Salazar for wine pairings, wine for the photo shoot, and helping to nurture Jill's relationship with food and wine over many years.

Thanks to Taylor Thompson for unconditional support and help with everything along the way.

# contents

# This book is for those who want to prepare downright delicious party food.

# INTRODUCTION

Whether for a backyard barbecue or an impromptu gathering, we develop our recipes around conscious cooking. That means serving dishes that are sustainably produced, but it also means not getting stressed about the details during prep. Our recipes and tips help you plan ahead, save time, save money, and stay healthy. Our book will inspire you to throw dinner parties more often.

During the years that we've been cooking together, we've learned that people feel better after they've eaten a lighter (but still insanely delicious and satisfying) meal. We've learned to cook food that is beneficial to our lives—both physically and mentally. That translates into a fabulous repertoire of dishes from a brunch menu filled with divine, dark leafy greens to an outstanding recipe for chocolate chip cookies. After all, we are mindful of our sweet tooth, too. We can show you how to make food that does right by the body while making your mouth water. When you eat healthfully, you feel good, and when you feel good, you look good!

Gather around a table. Clink glasses. Toast at the top of your lungs.

***Start here to party like a culinista.***

# WHAT'S A CULINISTA?

**Culinista**, a term coined for the personal chefs of The Dish's Dish (that's us), captures the essence of any confident home chef. A Culinista is the person at the center of every great party scene. She knows her way around the kitchen but isn't ashamed to use recipes or call her mother for help. A Culinista is also a guy who can make anything from a multicourse dinner for his girlfriend's parents to a lazy Sunday brunch. And if a big celebration with lots of friends is called for, a Culinista is on it—bells, whistles, and a few hors d'oeuvres should do it!

A Culinista is savvy about what she eats but doesn't obsess over every calorie. She strikes a balance between delicious, nutrient-rich foods that benefit her body and foods that are not quite as healthy, but might satisfy something else.

A Culinista makes a mindful effort to buy ingredients of which she knows the origin. She's educated about the best practices in agriculture and food production without being preachy. She's opinionated about food but doesn't stand on a soapbox.

Culinistas are environmentally conscious while acknowledging the need for convenience and easy chic, from grocery shopping to culinary technique. Culinistas are the masters of making healthful, eco-minded recipes with charm and elegance. They realize that being a host can have moments of stress but know not to let that ruin their good time!

### THE INSIDE SCOOP: WHAT JILL AND JOSIE REALLY EAT

We eat a plant-based diet, but make room for fish and other animal products that are ethically treated, sustainably raised, and prepared with a nod towards health and wellbeing. We recognize the dichotomy in the culinary world and in the media that simultaneously celebrates bacon fat French fries and vegan lunch boxes. Our core desire is to indulge and yet honor our bodies. We know we feel better when we opt for quinoa with kale and pine nuts over a cheeseburger. So, most of the time it's the whole grain and animal-friendly option. But sometimes we just crave a burger, so we enjoy the best quality meat we can get.

# ABOUT THIS BOOK

**Our menus** aim to give you the inspiration for glorious parties of your own making—from intimate get-togethers for a few close friends to blowout events—without getting bogged down by stress. A Culinista stays cool, calm, and collected! We have included a few notes and ideas that will make it easier for you to pull off an A+ spread.

## SPECIAL CONSIDERATIONS

Our book is divided into five chapters for five different kinds of parties. After all, there's a party to be had on any day of the week, for any occasion, and in any season. We invite you to party while the sun's still up, to party with just one other person, to party with your entire crew, to party at the very last minute, or simply, to party anytime, anywhere.

Each type of event offers its own set of variables. There's more or less prep time depending on the number of people and intricacy of dishes. Many daytime party items can be prepped the night before; after all, who wants to wake up at 6 a.m. to slice onions?! Our more international menus might involve a little more spice hunting—a worthy adventure. Some ingredients are hard to find out of season, but in season, you should be able to find everything at your local farmers' market—in abundance and cheap! Dinners for two have slightly more elaborate dishes, but because you only make two servings, they are totally doable. And those blowout parties will require the most work—but they also might be the most rewarding. Though we don't suggest that you make everything from the list of dishes, you could always turn these menus into a potluck by assigning your friends one or two items.

## PARTY SIZE

One of the first things that comes to mind when we plan a party is the guest list. Eight to ten is a nice start for a dinner party. It's a crowd, but not crowded. It's lively, but won't get you in trouble with the neighbors. Twenty people is certainly more involved—in terms of food preparation, grocery shopping, counter space, oven space, and seating arrangements—but still manageable.

We've geared most of the servings in our recipes for a party of ten. But this is of course loose, as everyone eats different amounts of food. And you may or may not make entire menus. For instance, although a recipe says it serves eight, if you choose to make the menu in its entirety, each dish can most likely stretch to serve ten. The serving for eight is based on if you made that dish alone. In our Party of Two menus, you might have leftovers for the next morning. Blowout party dishes are made to serve eight, but as we said, if you make all these dishes, you'll surely have plenty of food to go around. Try to base the quantity of food you make on your own appetites and those of your friends. And remember, everyone loves to take home leftovers.

## PLANNING TIPS

While creating our menus, we've listed the order in which you should start making each dish. Of course, as you get cooking, you'll want to make certain parts of one dish simultaneously with another. The order should help guide this process, making for the most efficient planning. Additionally, we've let you know when is the best time to make the always-until-now frantic outfit change. This will help you stay unstressed, knowing that you won't be answering the door in an apron and with an unwashed face.

We always keep in mind those dishes that can be made ahead, made fast, or made vegan. Some components of certain dishes can be made ahead and sometimes you can bang out the entire dish in advance (recipes marked (MA)). Some recipes are easy and quick to make ((S)). Some of our dishes are vegan ((V)) as listed and some can be made into vegan dishes by simply omitting one or two ingredients ((VO)). Many of our recipes fall into more than one of these categories so that you can reap the time-saving, health-rewarding, and stress-reducing benefits. Starting to sound pretty appetizing, huh?!

## PARTY TIME!

Before you even begin grocery shopping, make sure your broiler, oven, and burners are working, if you are not in the habit of cooking. Prior to cooking, take out the garbage and make sure you've got enough room to trash odds and ends in the appropriate places (carrot tops in compost, tofu package in recycling, etc.) as you go. Be sure all of your dishes are clean. Get the place ready for cooking! It'll only take a few minutes—you can do it!

As your guests start arriving, think about things from their point of view: They're nibbly and could use a glass of wine after a hard day's work. So, first things first: Put out some bites—our menus include some great appetizers—or prepare something simple such as popcorn or a cheese plate. Then, open a bottle of wine (check out our pairings, suggested to us by a dashing man in the biz). Done! Guests are taken care of for at least a half an hour. Now you can stop feeling like they are waiting for something. They're not! They are here to see you, to plug in with friends, and to enjoy themselves. So you should, too!

## PARTY CHECKLIST

• Chill your white and sparkling wine immediately upon arriving home from the market. Chuck the bottles in the freezer if you're short on time.
• Have enough plates, forks, knives, and spoons; don't worry if they don't all match, just alternate the patterns for more visual quirkiness.
• Buy some cute cocktail napkins.
• If there's one thing you do décor-wise, go buy flowers! It adds atmosphere to even the most boring room. If you have leftover fresh herbs they can act as your centerpiece. Make mini-bouquets in simple glasses or Ball jars.
• Set out all your glasses and create a bar area. Buy ice and remember to get some seltzer for those not drinking alcohol.
• Make a playlist. Load up your favorite tunes on a playlist that's at least two and a half hours long. If you aren't confident in doing this, ask that friend who loves to make mixes.
• Make sure your bathroom is clean and stocked. Don't embarrass your guests by making them ask for toilet paper!

# THE

## *culinista*

## KITCHEN

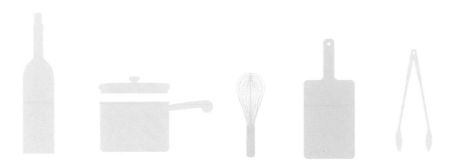

Knowing what's in your kitchen and having just a few chef's

tools on hand can make all the difference. Certain items

can dramatically improve your cooking experience as well as

the taste and presentation of your dishes. Some of these

items may seem specialty, but trust us: once you start using

them, you won't want to put them down.

[ ABSOLUTELY ESSENTIAL ]

# *tools*

---

### MICROPLANE:

This tool can save time when shredding hard cheeses, mincing garlic, and zesting citrus.

### MANDOLINE:

They come in a variety of price ranges. Look for one that slices at varying widths and has a julienne attachment. Be sure to take precautions—steady the mandoline on a proper surface, and keep your hands away from the blade. We both have inexpensive versions that work great!

### CUTTING BOARD:

Try to get as large a surface as you can fit comfortably in your kitchen. Cutting boards help prevent injury, protect your kitchen surfaces from damage, and keep bacteria at bay. Be sure to thoroughly wash your cutting board after prepping raw meats on it.

### PEELER:

A peeler not only works on your carrots and potatoes, but you can also use it to peel squash and other hard vegetables. It's safer than using your knife and saves tons of time.

### GOOD KNIFE:

Your knife needs to be comfortable in your hands and have a sharp edge. Though a personal splurge item for Josie, you can accomplish this at various price ranges.

[ SERIOUSLY GOOD IDEAS ]

# *tools*

----------------------------------------------------------------

### SQUEEZE BOTTLES:

These are very inexpensive and very useful! Keep one for olive oil,
one for water, and a few empty ones into which you can pour
sauces and vinaigrettes.

### IMMERSION BLENDER:

Jill got an immersion blender (also called a hand blender) a few years
ago and uses it constantly. Purée soups, blend salad dressings, and
make smooth dips with it—it's genius! Of course, the same thing can be
accomplished with a food processor or standard blender, too.

### GRILL OR GRILL PAN:

Something about the slightly charred, caramelized flavor of food
makes those taste buds go crazy. It's also one way to cook food that
adds lots of flavor without adding much fat. However, remember to
keep your grill clean, as the buildup is not good for the body.

### BAKEWARE:

We often use a rimmed baking sheet, a 9x13-inch baking dish, and
ramekins for many of the recipes in the book. They are useful standards
to have around.

• • •

*For any kitchen tools,* remember to buy the best quality that you
can afford. This will minimize the amount of useless, flimsy equipment
that ends up in the trash. Think about how many times a cheap can
opener has gone wonky on you.

IT STARTS WITH

# ingredients

We always opt for:

**WHOLE-GRAIN OVER OVERLY-REFINED PRODUCTS:**

The extra vitamins and fiber are an easy switch that keep you sated.

**ORGANIC OVER CONVENTIONALLY FARMED PRODUCTS:**

Many foods are now available as USDA-certified organic. We support the effort, though there are still some kinks to be worked out in this market. We also enjoy fruits and veggies without the USDA stamp that are locally grown by small-scale farmers who put care and attention into their products. Try to buy organic varieties of peaches, apples, bell peppers, celery, nectarines, strawberries, cherries, pears, grapes, spinach, lettuce, potatoes, corn and its by-products, as well as soy and its by-products, because conventionally, these are sprayed the heaviest or absorb more pesticides through their thin skins. Regardless of growing practices, be sure to buy your food in good condition and store it properly.

**HUMANELY- AND SUSTAINABLY-RAISED SEAFOOD, POULTRY, MEAT:**

When consuming animals, be sure that you purchase them from farmers and fisherman who treat them humanely during their lives. Avoid facilities that rely on overcrowding and overuse of antibiotics. This mistreatment not only harms the animal but also has ill effects on us and on the environment. Instead, choose meat that is free range, grass fed, and antibiotic free.

**PLANT-BASED MEALS OVER ANIMAL-BASED MEALS:**

Minimizing animal consumption has positive effects on your body and the planet. By going easy on animal intake, we're doing our part to preserve our environment, take care of our bodies, and open up to a world of delicious, plant-based foods. Get your protein through beans, quinoa, tofu, and nuts. Many of our recipes provide a great blueprint!

[ A FEW SPECIFICS ]

## *pantry*

- - - - - - - - - - - - - - - - - - - - - - - - - - - - - - - - - - - - - - - - - - - -

### ORGANIC WHOLE WHEAT PASTRY FLOUR

Instead of all-purpose flour, try whole wheat pastry flour. It has
a lighter, more delicate texture than plain whole wheat flour due
to its lower protein content. We generally use it for baking.
You can try substituting plain whole wheat flour or 1:1 mix of
whole-wheat and unbleached all-purpose flour if you cannot find
whole wheat pastry flour.

### TURBINADO OR RAW SUGAR

Unless otherwise stated, use this type of sugar to get our results.
Granulated sugar can be used in a pinch, but your results will be
slightly different and it's less healthy.

### AGAVE SYRUP

We use the darker amber version because it has a more
nuanced flavor that we love.

### FLAKY SEA SALT

Flaky sea salts, such as Maldon, provide a perfect finish for any dish—
from a grilled vegetable and pesto pizza to chocolate chip cookies.
We use fine sea salt for everyday cooking. Remember that salt is
generally to taste. Low-salt dieters can add various spices and even
lemon juice to trick the taste buds into consuming less salt.

### TRUFFLE SALT

A little truffle flavor makes everything gourmet. There are quite a few
dishes in these menus that become a bases-loaded home run with the
addition of truffle salt. Try it on the orrechiette salad (page 95), or the
baked eggs with spinach (page 149). Bet it'd be great in the polenta
(page 32) and the wheatberry salad (page 127), too.

### OLIVE OIL COOKING SPRAY

Lots of distribution, not a lot of oil. Make your own by pouring olive oil into a food-safe spray bottle.

### EXTRA-VIRGIN OLIVE OIL

Have two bottles on hand—one inexpensive one and one fine. The inexpensive bottle is for cooking, and the pricier, more flavorful bottle is for finishing dishes, such as drizzling a little over a soup or salad—give it that extra love!

### COCONUT OIL

Adds nutty flavor. Though it is high in saturated fat, your body burns it more easily than animal-based saturated fat. Plus, by using coconut oil, you don't need as much fat in volume per recipe. It's also an antiviral and antifungal food, helping with yeast levels in the body.

### SPROUTED GRAIN INGREDIENTS WHERE POSSIBLE

These are easier to digest, have more nutrients and flavor, and satisfy hunger better. Look for sprouted grain bread, bagels, english muffins, and more.

### FRESH SPICES

Half a teaspoon of cayenne pepper can go from potent if it's new to tasteless if it is too old. We suggest buying spices in small amounts. There are some wonderful online and in-store sources for spices where they're available for purchase by the quarter-ounce—sometimes in places you'd least expect, so ask around!

### MILK

Unless we call for a specific type of milk, you can use any milk that suits your diet. Almond milk, rice milk, soy milk, hemp milk, and any variety of cow's or goat's milk will warrant slightly different results depending on fat content and naked taste. We encourage you to try a few varieties until you find one that suits you.

### PARMESAN

We think cheese is one of those items worth the splurge and Parmesan is no exception. Look for a good quality Parmesan, such as Parmigiano-Reggiano, to use in these recipes.

[ WHERE'D YOU GET THAT?! ]

# sourcing

Selecting the right ingredients is just as important to us as the cooking and enjoyment of them. There is a whole world beyond your local supermarket. Using the internet and farmers' markets, you'll find all kinds of items and ingredients to make your party more special, more meaningful, and tastier!

We aren't the most frequent meat eaters, but when we do dive in, it comes from a trusted source. Buy meat at your local farmers market and get to know the people who are raising the animals. Find out about their slaughter practices. If you can't track down a trustworthy source for your meat before your party, you could skip the meat recipes completely. Our menus are perfectly delicious without them.

Meat is not the only food group that warrants special attention. Vegetables can get doused with harmful pesticides to keep bugs from eroding the crop, or they can be genetically modified from the get-go. We encourage you to speak with your local produce purveyors at the market to ensure that your vegetables are as pure as possible.

If you don't have a farmers' market near you, try to buy organic items in the grocery store. We know these items can be more expensive. But think about it: They are going into your body. Your brain will be functioning from this fuel. Your muscles and organs will be seeking vital nutrients from these meals. And, you might find that organic foods are simply more flavorful.

• • •

*If you want to learn more about where your food comes from*, we suggest some books, films, and websites that have made a lasting impression on us in our Sources (page 264). We've also included a list of places where you can get certain hard-to-find ingredients.

*anytime*

*parties*

***Our experiences are as eclectic as our taste buds***—from Josie's roots in Jamaica to Jill's extended stay in Madagascar—and sometimes we can't help but add a little culture and timeliness into each dish. Whether communing with friends that you haven't seen in a while over the holidays, throwing a fiesta-style birthday party, making a congratulatory dinner with here-today ingredients, welcoming out-of-towners with a Mediterranean meal, or celebrating a completed deadline with the sunburst flavor of a tomato picked in late August—your guests will jam to these menus.

Maybe you want to celebrate spring; maybe you want to use some of those quirky spices you've just smuggled in from your last trip to Mexico. Or maybe the mood for a stir-fry strikes up reason for an entire fête. Whatever it is, there's always a reason to party. The menus listed in this double-disc chapter are meant to be made anytime, anywhere. Some ingredients may take a little sourcing and some might be better-made in season, but they always evoke the same "we're not worthy!" response from groupie guests.

*xo, Jill & Josie*

# menu

*anytime*

| | SPEEDY | MAKE AHEAD | VEGAN | VEGAN FLEX |
|---|---|---|---|---|
| *slow-baked red bell peppers* | | MA | V | |
| *whole roasted fish stuffed with herbs* | | | | |
| *creamy basil polenta with buttons + shiitakes* | | | | |
| *semolina + orange cake* | | MA | | |

## WINE PAIRING

When pairing peppers, fresh fish, and herbs, look to the Greek isles for refreshment—snappy Moschofilero or succulent Assyrtiko are sure to make your meze memorable.

## COOKING ORDER

*1.* cake

*2.* bell peppers

*3.* fish

*4.* polenta

## WARDROBE CHANGE

Change after cooking the polenta. Stir in the pecorino and basil over low heat to finish the dish just before your guests arrive.

TOTAL TIME: 1 HOUR, 20 MINUTES / SERVES 6

# slow-baked *red bell peppers*

4 red bell peppers

2 tablespoons red wine vinegar

2 tablespoons extra virgin olive oil

1 tablespoon turbinado or raw sugar

1/2 teaspoon fine grain sea salt

1/4 teaspoon freshly ground black pepper

1 clove garlic, minced

Olives, marinated mushrooms, bread, etc., for serving

• Preheat the oven to 375°F. Seed the bell peppers and slice lengthwise into 1/2-inch batons.

• Place the peppers in a bowl and combine with the vinegar, olive oil, sugar, salt, pepper, and garlic.

• Transfer to a 9x13-inch baking dish and cover with aluminum foil. Bake for 1 hour. Let cool and serve warm, room temperature, or cold.

• Serve alongside the olives, mushrooms, and bread.

## notes

**You can make this dish one day in advance;** store in the refrigerator. Reheat, covered with aluminum foil, in the oven for 15 minutes at 350°F.

**These peppers are also great** added to a salad or sandwich.

TOTAL TIME: 45 MINUTES / SERVES 8

# *whole roasted fish*
## *stuffed with herbs*

2 (2 1/2-pound) red snappers, heads on, scaled, gutted, and finned

10 sprigs fresh thyme

1 lemon, cut into 6 slices

4 tablespoons chopped fresh flat-leaf parsley

4 bay leaves

2 tablespoons extra virgin olive oil

Flaky sea salt, such as Maldon

Freshly ground black pepper

4 cups tender salad greens, such as arugula or spinach

Fine extra virgin olive oil, for drizzling

• Preheat the oven to 425°F. Slice the fish open on the underside, cutting from under the head to 1 inch from the tail. Stuff each fish with 5 thyme sprigs, 3 lemon slices, 2 tablespoons parsley, and 2 bay leaves. Drizzle the olive oil over the fish and sprinkle with salt.

• Line a rimmed baking sheet with parchment or aluminum foil. Lay the fish side by side on the sheet. Bake for 30 minutes or until the flesh is white, somewhat opaque, and flakes easily. Crack a bit of black pepper over the fish. Serve with salad greens on the side, drizzled with olive oil.

## *notes*

*Be sure to get the freshest possible fish* so that you can display the results with pride. Nice firm skin, bright eyes, and red gills are signs of fresh whole fish.

*Ask your fishmonger* to scale, gut, and trim the fins off the fish for you.

*Josie favors red snapper* thanks to her Caribbean roots, but other medium-size whole fish work well in this recipe, too.

TOTAL TIME: 40 MINUTES / SERVES 10

# creamy basil polenta
## with buttons + shiitakes

1 cup dried shiitake mushrooms

2 tablespoons extra virgin olive oil

1 1/2 cups chopped onions

1 clove garlic, minced

3 1/2 cups sliced button mushrooms

1/2 teaspoon fine grain sea salt

3 cups milk

3 cups water

1 tablespoon fresh thyme leaves

1 cup instant or quick polenta

1/2 cup freshly grated Pecorino Romano cheese

1/2 cup fresh basil leaves cut into a chiffonade

• Bring a small pot of water to a boil. Add the dried shiitakes and continue to boil until the shiitakes have been reconstituted, about 5 minutes. Drain off the water and reserve the mushrooms. If your shiitakes have stems, remove and discard them. Slice the shiitake caps and set aside.

• Heat the olive oil in a large saucepan over medium heat; sauté the onions, garlic, button mushrooms, and salt until the onions soften, about 10 minutes. Add the milk, water, and thyme. Simmer for 5 minutes over low heat.

• Sprinkle in the polenta while stirring. Continue to stir while simmering for 5 to 10 minutes. The polenta should be soft with no lumps. Remove from the heat. Stir in the pecorino, shiitakes, and basil and serve.

## notes

**Dried mushrooms** have a stronger flavor, which this dish needs to truly bring the flavors together.

**Polenta** comes in a variety of cooking types: 1-minute, 2-minute, 5-minute, or 30 to 45 minutes. Save time by getting the 1-, 2-, or 5-minute varieties.

**Dry polenta** is usually found near the pasta section in your market. This is not the ready-to-eat variety found in the refrigerated section.

**Don't know how to make a chiffonade?** See Quick Reference (page 256).

TOTAL TIME: 1 HOUR / MAKES ONE 9-INCH CAKE, ABOUT 12 SERVINGS

# semolina + orange *cake*

Olive oil cooking spray

1 cup whole wheat pastry flour

1 cup semolina flour

1 teaspoon baking powder

1/4 teaspoon fine grain sea salt

1 cup extra virgin olive oil

1 teaspoon pure vanilla extract

1 tablespoon grated orange zest

5 large eggs

1 cup turbinado or raw sugar

**ORANGE SYRUP:**

3 tablespoons turbinado or raw sugar

1/3 cup fresh orange juice (from about 1 orange)

• Preheat the oven to 350°F. Spray a 9-inch cake pan with olive oil spray. In a bowl, mix together the flours, baking powder, and salt.

• In a separate bowl, mix the olive oil with vanilla and orange zest.

• Crack the eggs into a third, large bowl. Whisk the eggs for 5 minutes on high with an electric mixer. After the first minute, gradually beat in the sugar. After 5 minutes, the finished eggs should be fairly silky and flow like a thin ribbon when you lift the beater and shake it. Add a third of the flour mixture to the eggs and whisk for 5 seconds to incorporate. Add half of the oil mixture and mix again for 5 seconds. Repeat with another third of the flour and mix. Mix in the remaining olive oil, and the last third of the flour mixture.

• Pour the batter into the prepared pan and smooth out the top. Bake until brown on top and a tester (a knife or a skewer) inserted into center comes out clean, about 40 minutes.

• MEANWHILE, MAKE THE ORANGE SYRUP: Boil the sugar with orange juice, letting it reduce until syrupy, about 3 minutes.

• After the cake has cooled for 5 minutes, remove it from the pan and pour on the syrup, spreading it all over the top of the cake. Let cool and serve.

## notes

*Store any unused semolina flour* in the fridge, inside an airtight plastic bag. It tends to go stale faster than other flours.

*Serve with* whipped cream or jam.

*This cake is great* in the morning alongside ginger or spice tea.

*This cake can also be made* in a Bundt pan. Cooking time would be increased by about 5 minutes.

*This cake can be made one day in advance.* Store refrigerated in an airtight container. Remove from the fridge a few hours before serving and let the cake come to room temp.

# menu

| | SPEEDY | MAKE AHEAD | VEGAN | VEGAN FLEX |
|---|---|---|---|---|
| *fava bean pesto bruschetta* | | MA | | |
| *butternut squash + spinach lasagna* | | MA | | |
| *chile garlic broccolini* | S | | | VF |
| *apple raisin tart with pecan crust* | | MA | V | |

## WINE PAIRING

Italy abounds with regional white wines perfect for dishes like these. Seek out honey-scented Fruilanos from northern Italy, or foxy Campanian whites like Greco di Tufo or Falanghina.

## COOKING ORDER

*1.* tart

*2.* lasagna

*3.* bruschetta

*4.* broccolini

## WARDROBE CHANGE

Do everything except sauté the broccolini, then change. Leave the lasagna in a warm oven until after the guests arrive.

TOTAL TIME: 30 MINUTES / SERVES 8

# *fava bean pesto* **bruschetta**

3 cups shucked fava beans
(about 4 pounds of pods)

1/2 cup walnut pieces

1/4 cup freshly grated
Parmesan cheese

Zest and juice of 1/2 lemon

1 clove garlic

2 tablespoons chopped fresh
flat-leaf parsley

1/4 cup extra virgin olive oil

1/2 teaspoon fine grain sea salt

1/4 teaspoon freshly ground
black pepper

1 whole grain baguette

• Place a pot of water over high heat and bring to a boil. Add the fava beans and boil for 5 minutes. Drain and immerse in cold water. Peel the beans from their individual casings and set them aside.

• Blend the walnuts, Parmesan, lemon zest and juice, and the garlic until smooth in a food processor. Add half of the fava beans and all of the parsley to the food processor and blend for another 10 seconds. Try to keep it a little chunky with identifiable pieces of fava bean. Stir in the remaining favas and the olive oil. Season with salt and pepper.

• Cut the bread into 1/2-inch slices. Using a grill or broiler, cook the bread until just lightly browned.

Serve the pesto alongside the bread, or spread the pesto directly onto the slices.

## *notes*

**Use frozen favas,** peas, or edamame if you can't find fresh fava beans.

**This pesto can be made up to one week in advance;** store covered in the refrigerator. Toast the bread just before serving.

TOTAL TIME: 2 HOURS  / SERVES 12

# butternut squash + spinach *lasagna*

1 cup heavy cream

1 teaspoon dried lavender

1 onion, chopped

1 teaspoon extra virgin olive oil

2 tablespoons whole wheat pastry flour

2 cups milk

1/8 teaspoon ground nutmeg

2 teaspoons fresh thyme leaves

2 cups plus 1 tablespoon water

1/2 teaspoon fine grain sea salt

1/8 teaspoon freshly ground black pepper

12 ounces baby spinach

1 cup freshly grated Parmesan cheese

1 pound ricotta cheese

1 (1-pound) package fresh or no-boil lasagna sheets

1 butternut squash (2 to 3 pounds), peeled and cut into 1/2-inch slices (about 4 1/2 cups)

1 cup shredded mozzarella cheese

• Preheat the oven to 350°F. In a small saucepan over low heat, simmer the cream and lavender for 10 minutes. Remove from heat and let the lavender steep for an additional 10 minutes. Pour the cream and lavender into a blender and blend till smooth.

• In a separate saucepan over medium heat, sauté the onion with the olive oil. Stir in the flour and cook for another minute. Add the milk, nutmeg, thyme, and 2 cups water. Simmer and stir until the mixture thickens, about 15 minutes. Add the salt and pepper. Pour the lavender cream into the milk mixture, stirring to combine; set aside.

• Heat a sauté pan over medium heat. Add the spinach and 1 tablespoon water. Cook, stirring, until the spinach is just wilted, about 4 minutes. Let the spinach cool slightly, strain, and set aside.

• In a small bowl, mix 1/2 cup Parmesan with all of the ricotta.

• In a 9x13-inch baking dish, pour enough milk sauce to cover the bottom of the pan, then place a layer of pasta followed by a little more sauce. Then layer the butternut squash, spinach, and ricotta mix. Follow with sauce, another layer of pasta, and more sauce. Repeat the butternut squash, spinach, and ricotta. Place another layer of pasta on top; cover with remaining milk sauce and then top off with the remaining Parmesan and all of the mozzarella.

• Bake, covered with aluminum foil, for 1 hour. Then remove the foil and broil to brown the top, 2 to 3 minutes. Let cool slightly before serving.

## notes

*Lavender buds* may be found with the spices or in the baking section of specialty markets. Check out our Sources (page 264) if you have trouble finding them.

*If you want to skip the step* of blending the lavender with the cream, you can strain the lavender flowers out after it's steeped. This will yield a milder lavender flavor.

*You can make the lasagna* one day in advance; store covered in the refrigerator. Reheat in a 325°F oven for 30 to 45 minutes.

TOTAL TIME: 15 MINUTES / SERVES 10

S VF

# *chile garlic broccolini*

1/2 teaspoon fine grain sea salt

3 bunches broccolini (about 2 pounds)

1 tablespoon extra virgin olive oil

2 cloves garlic, minced

1 1/2 teaspoons red chile pepper flakes

2 tablespoons freshly grated Parmesan cheese

• Bring a medium pot of water to a boil; add the salt. Add the broccolini and cook for 1 1/2 minutes. Remove to an ice bath and submerge the broccolini until cool. Drain and set aside.

• Heat the olive oil in a sauté pan over medium heat; sauté the garlic and chile flakes for 1 minute. Increase the heat to high, add the broccolini, and cook, stirring, for about 4 minutes, or until broccolini is hot and lightly blistered. Remove from heat and sprinkle with Parmesan before serving.

## *notes*

***Omit the Parmesan*** to make this a vegan dish.

***A quick blanch*** keeps the veggies a vibrant green. See Quick Reference (page 255) for more information about blanching.

TOTAL TIME: 90 MINUTES PLUS COOLING / SERVES 12

# *apple raisin tart* with pecan crust

**CRUST:**

1 1/2 cups pecan halves

1 cup whole wheat pastry flour

3 tablespoons turbinado or raw sugar

1/4 teaspoon ground cinnamon

1/2 teaspoon fine grain sea salt

1/4 cup coconut oil

4 to 5 tablespoons water

**FILLING:**

1/2 cup golden raisins

1/4 cup dry white wine or water

1 tablespoon fresh orange juice

2 tablespoons plus 1 1/2 teaspoons rum

1/4 cup plus 1 tablespoon turbinado or raw sugar

1 1/2 to 2 pounds apples, cored and quartered but not peeled (about 4 medium apples)

2 tablespoons fresh lemon juice (from about 1 lemon)

1/4 teaspoon ground cinnamon

1/8 teaspoon ground nutmeg

1/8 teaspoon ground allspice

1 tablespoon coconut oil

• MAKE THE CRUST: Preheat the oven to 400°F. Place the pecans and flour in a food processor and blend until it looks like coarse cornmeal. Add the sugar, cinnamon, and salt; process 10 seconds. Then add coconut oil; process 10 seconds. Add water as needed if the dough needs more binding. Turn the dough out of the food processor and press into a 10-inch tart pan. Trim the excess. Refrigerate for 15 minutes covered in plastic wrap.

• MAKE THE FILLING: In a small saucepan, bring the raisins, wine, orange juice, 1 1/2 teaspoons rum, and 1 tablespoon sugar to a boil over medium heat. Reduce the heat and simmer for 20 minutes. Strain off and reserve the excess liquid; reserve the raisins.

• Meanwhile, on a cutting board, slice the apple quarters thinly, about 1/8 inch thick. Spread the raisins out in an even layer on the bottom of the crust. Lay the apples on top of the raisins.

• Mix together the reserved liquid, lemon juice, cinnamon, nutmeg, allspice, 1/4 cup sugar, 2 tablespoons rum, and the coconut oil. Pour this mixture over the apples.

• Bake the tart until the crust is crisp and the apples wilted, about 45 minutes. Let cool before serving.

## notes

*If you don't have a food processor,* crush the pecans with the back of a heavy pan and continue to mix in the ingredients by hand.

*Use a pie pan* if a tart pan is not available.

*Work quickly with the apples* to prevent them from browning.

*Have extra pie dough?* Make little cookies with any remaining dough by shaping into balls, pressing a thumbprint into the middle, and filling with jam or extra raisins. Bake for 15 minutes at 350°F.

*Make the pie a day one day in advance;* store covered in the refrigerator. Reheat in a 300°F oven until warm.

# menu

| | SPEEDY | MAKE AHEAD | VEGAN | VEGAN FLEX |
|---|---|---|---|---|
| *kimchi scallion pancakes* | | MA | | VF |
| *red miso bbq pork with pineapple jam* | | MA | | |
| *pepita-crusted tofu* | | MA | V | |
| *mango chile cabbage slaw* | | MA | V | |
| *lychee, honeydew + mint sorbet* | | MA | V | |

## WINE PAIRING

When spice plays a major role on the menu, consider Riesling. Many Washington State Rieslings have the careful balance of fruit and fresh acidity that works just as well with mango as it does with BBQ pork—Kung Fu Girl is one of our favorites.

## COOKING ORDER

*1.* sorbet

*2.* bbq pork

*3.* tofu

*4.* slaw

*5.* pancakes

## WARDROBE CHANGE

Make everything; keep tofu and pork warm in a 250°F oven while you change. If you feel like being interactive in the kitchen, you can make the pancakes with your guests.

TOTAL TIME: 45 MINUTES / MAKES 24 PANCAKES

MA VF

# kimchi scallion *pancakes*

**DIPPING SAUCE:**

1/2 cup reduced-sodium soy sauce

2 tablespoons sesame oil

1 tablespoon red chile pepper flakes

2 scallions, chopped

2 teaspoons grated fresh ginger

**PANCAKES:**

5 scallions, cut into 1/2-inch pieces

3/4 cup chopped kimchi

2 tablespoons black sesame seeds

3/4 cup potato starch

3/4 cup whole wheat pastry flour

5 cloves garlic, minced

2 tablespoons hot chili sauce (such as Sriracha)

1 large egg

3/4 cup water

1/4 teaspoon fine grain sea salt

Olive oil cooking spray

• MAKE THE DIPPING SAUCE: Stir together the soy sauce, sesame oil, chile flakes, scallions, and ginger. Set aside.

• MAKE THE PANCAKES: Mix together all ingredients except the cooking spray.

• Heat a skillet over medium heat. Spray with olive oil and add 1 heaping spoonful of batter per pancake. Sear for about 3 minutes per side over medium-low heat. They should be slightly brown. Repeat with the remaining batter. Serve with the dipping sauce.

## notes

*Swap the egg* with an egg replacer for a vegan dish.

*Kimchi* is usually kept refrigerated and looks a little like spicy sauerkraut. You can find it in Asian food stores.

*Sriracha sauce* is a hot sauce from Thailand. Adjust the amount to add more/less heat to your pancakes.

*The dipping sauce* can be made one day in advance; keep covered in the refrigerator.

*These always get rave reviews*. And, you can make extra batter and serve some up for lunch the next day!

TOTAL TIME: 6 HOURS INCLUDING MARINATING / SERVES 10 TO 12

# red miso *bbq pork* with pineapple jam

4 pounds boneless pork butt, rinsed

**RED MISO MARINADE:**

2 tablespoons grated fresh ginger

5 scallions, chopped

10 cloves garlic, minced

1/2 cup mirin

1/4 cup red miso

1/4 cup hoisin sauce

1 teaspoon red chile pepper flakes

1/2 teaspoon fine grain sea salt

1 tablespoon sesame oil

**JAM:**

1 pineapple, peeled and cored

1 vanilla bean

1 cup turbinado or raw sugar

MA

• Cut the pork into 2-inch chunks.

• MAKE THE MARINADE: In a large bowl, mix together all the ingredients. Place pork and marinade in a closed container and place in the refrigerator to marinate for at least 3 hours or overnight.

• Preheat the oven to 325°F. Arrange the pork in a 9x13-inch baking dish and pour the marinade over the pork. Cover the dish with foil. Cook the pork for 2 1/2 hours or until tender and easy to pull apart.

• MEANWHILE, MAKE THE JAM: Shred the pineapple with a cheese grater. Split the vanilla bean in half lengthwise and scrape out the seeds; reserve the seeds and pod. Place the pineapple, sugar, and vanilla bean pod and seeds in a large nonreactive pot over medium-low heat and simmer, 1 hour, stirring occasionally. It should be thick and jam-like. Let cool to room temperature.

• Shred the pork with a fork onto a serving platter and serve with pineapple jam on the side.

## notes

**Pork butt** is actually the upper part of the pork shoulder, so the "butt" and the cut called the "shoulder" are often used interchangeably. Any cut from the shoulder would do for this recipe; just be sure to purchase the boneless, leaner pieces if you have the choice.

**Red miso** is usually kept refrigerated near the tofu in the grocery. It's also sometimes found in the Asian or international food aisle.

**There is very little cooking liquid** when baking the pork. If the bottom of the pan starts to burn, check your oven temperature and add about 1/2 cup of water.

**The jam can be made in advance;** keep in a sealed container for up to 1 week, refrigerated. The pork can be finished one day in advance; cover and refrigerate, then reheat in a 350°F oven in a foil-covered baking dish until hot, about 25 minutes.

**If you also plan on making Petipa-Crusted Tofu** (page 46), remember to make extra marinade.

# pepita-crusted tofu

2 pounds extra-firm tofu (about 2 packages), well drained

1/2 cup Red Miso Marinade (pages 44–45)

1/2 cup untoasted pepitas

2 tablespoons maple syrup

1/4 teaspoon cayenne pepper

1 teaspoon turmeric

2 tablespoons sesame seeds

• Slice each pound of tofu into 16 squares. Combine the marinade and tofu and marinate, covered, for 1 hour in the refrigerator.

• Preheat the oven to 350°F. In a small bowl, toss the pepitas with maple syrup, cayenne, turmeric, and sesame seeds.

• Remove the tofu from the marinade and let the excess drip off. Lay the tofu flat on a baking sheet. Top the tofu with the pepita mix. Bake for 30 minutes. Serve hot.

## notes

**Press the tofu** between paper or cloth towels to rid it of excess water before marinating.

**Pepitas** are green pumpkin seeds, often pre-toasted. Look for untoasted for this recipe.

**The marinade can be made** one day in advance; store covered in the refrigerator. Don't add the tofu until the day of your event.

TOTAL TIME: 25 MINUTES / SERVES 10

MA V

# mango chile *cabbage slaw*

1 head napa cabbage, shredded thinly

2 cups sliced almonds, toasted lightly (see Quick Reference, page 262)

2 mangoes, peeled and sliced into thin wedges

**DRESSING:**

1 tablespoon red chile pepper flakes

1/2 cup brown rice vinegar

1/2 cup vegetable oil

1 tablespoon turbinado or raw sugar

1/4 cup fresh lime juice (from about 4 limes)

3/4 teaspoon fine grain sea salt

• Mix together the cabbage, almonds, and mango in a large bowl.

• MAKE THE DRESSING: Whisk the chile flakes, rice vinegar, vegetable oil, sugar, lime juice, and salt together in a small bowl.

• Add the dressing to the cabbage mixture and toss.

## notes

*If you can't find brown rice vinegar,* you use more easily found rice vinegar.

*You can prep all of the components* a day in advance; store them separately and refrigerate the cabbage, mangoes, and dressing. An hour before the party, mix everything together.

PARTY LIKE A CULINISTA

TOTAL TIME: 15 MINUTES PLUS FREEZING / MAKES 1 QUART, ABOUT 8 SERVINGS

# lychee, honeydew + mint *sorbet*

1/2 cup water

1/2 cup turbinado or raw sugar

1 (13 1/2-ounce) can lychees, drained

3 to 4 cups chopped honeydew melon

1/8 teaspoon fine grain sea salt

1 1/2 teaspoons fresh lime juice (from about 1/2 lime)

1/4 cup fresh mint leaves

• In a small saucepan over medium heat, heat the water and sugar together until the sugar melts; 3 minutes. Let cool.

• Working in batches, puree everything together in a blender, using half of the sugar syrup, until smooth. Depending on the sweetness of the fruit, you may add more sugar syrup.

• Freeze according to ice cream maker instructions.

## notes

**Use fresh lychees** if you are lucky enough to find them. If you live near a Chinatown, you'll find them there; you can also find them at specialty markets from time to time. Peel and pit the fruit and use the juicy flesh. Canned lychees are found in the Asian section of your grocery.

**This can be a granita** if you don't have an ice cream maker: Follow freezing instructions for Cherry Watermelon Granita (page 84).

**Can be made in advance;** the sorbet will keep for up to 1 month in the freezer.

# menu

| | SPEEDY | MAKE AHEAD | VEGAN | VEGAN FLEX |
|---|---|---|---|---|
| *chile lime almonds* | S | MA | V | |
| *herbed heirloom tomato salad* | S | | V | |
| *roasted vegetable enchiladas* | | MA | | VF |
| *horchata pops* | | MA | V | |

***Party Extra: Play up the Mexican theme of this menu with a piñata.*** Order one online and stuff it with anything from Kinder Hippos to Schleich plastic toys to bouncy balls or whoopee cushions.

| WINE PAIRING | COOKING ORDER | WARDROBE CHANGE |
|---|---|---|
| Pick up some ice-cold pilsner and plenty of it for this Mexican-influenced spread. If you are in the mood for vino, grab a Chilean Sauvignon Blanc from the Leyda Valley or one of Argentina's bargain-priced Malbecs. | *1.* pops<br>*2.* almonds<br>*3.* enchiladas<br>*4.* salad | Do everything but bake the enchiladas, then change. The enchiladas can go in the oven when guests start to arrive. |

TOTAL TIME: 20 MINUTES / SERVES 8

S MA V

# *chile lime almonds*

*1 pound whole raw almonds*

*1/2 teaspoon cayenne pepper*

*1 teaspoon fine grain sea salt*

*2 teaspoons extra virgin olive oil*

*1 tablespoon grated lime zest, packed*

*2 tablespoons fresh lime juice (from about 2 limes)*

• Preheat the oven to 375°F. Mix together the almonds, cayenne, salt, and olive oil in a bowl. Spread the mixture onto a rimmed baking sheet.

• Roast the almonds for 10 to 15 minutes in the oven, until they are browned and crisp. Stir them halfway through the cooking time.

• Remove the tray from the oven and add the lime zest and juice while quickly stirring the almonds. Let them cool completely on the tray.

*notes*

*We love using unpeeled almonds* for this recipe, but peeled ones are fine, too.

*These almonds can be made* up to one week in advance. Store in an airtight container.

TOTAL TIME: 20 MINUTES / SERVES 10

S V

# *herbed heirloom tomato* **salad**

*6 medium assorted heirloom tomatoes, sliced into wedges*

*2 seedless cucumbers, chopped*

*1/2 cup chopped fresh flat-leaf parsley*

*1/4 cup chopped fresh cilantro*

*1/4 cup chopped fresh oregano*

*1 1/2 tablespoons Dijon mustard*

*1/3 cup fine extra virgin olive oil*

*1/3 cup white wine vinegar*

*1/2 teaspoon fine grain sea salt*

*1/4 teaspoon freshly ground black pepper*

• Toss together the tomatoes, cucumbers, parsley, cilantro, and oregano in a salad bowl.

• In a small bowl, whisk together the Dijon, olive oil, and vinegar. Season with salt and pepper. Drizzle the dressing over the salad and toss everything together.

## *notes*

**Remember that heirloom tomatoes** come in all shapes and sizes; get as many medium to small ones as you can—it will make your salad gorgeous!

**Seedless cucumbers** such as the hothouse or English cucumber variety contain smaller seeds, so tiny they won't be noticeable in the salad.

**A restaurant in Manhattan** used to serve a similar dish. When they took it off the menu, Jill almost fell off of her bar stool. Luckily, we've been able to recreate it.

TOTAL TIME: 1 HOUR, 35 MINUTES / SERVES 12

# roasted vegetable *enchiladas*

**VEGETABLE FILLING:**

1 zucchini, diced large

1 medium eggplant, diced large

1 yellow bell pepper, diced

1 red bell pepper, diced

1 large yellow onion, diced

3 tablespoons extra virgin olive oil

1/4 teaspoon fine grain sea salt

Olive oil cooking spray

18 corn tortillas

**SAUCE:**

1 teaspoon extra virgin olive oil

6 cloves garlic, minced

1 cup diced red onion

1 1/2 teaspoons chili powder

1 teaspoon ground cumin

1 teaspoon ground coriander

1 (16-ounce) can fire-roasted diced tomatoes (about 2 cups)

1 tablespoon dried oregano

1/4 teaspoon fine grain sea salt

1 cup shredded cheddar cheese

1 cup shredded Monterey jack cheese

*continued*

• Preheat the oven to 425°F. Line 2 rimmed baking sheets with parchment paper.

• MAKE THE FILLING: Toss the zucchini, eggplant, bell peppers, and onion in a large bowl with the olive oil and salt. Spread the mixture evenly on the prepared baking sheets. Roast the vegetables in the oven for 25 minutes, stirring occasionally.

• Meanwhile, spray a sauté pan with olive oil and, one by one or as many that can fit in a single layer, heat the tortillas over medium-low heat, about 30 seconds per side. Set aside, covered.

• MAKE THE SAUCE: Place a medium saucepan over high heat, add the olive oil, and sauté the garlic and red onion for 3 minutes. The garlic and onions will brown considerably. Add the chili powder, cumin, and coriander and cook another 30 seconds, stirring. Add the tomatoes, oregano, and salt. Stir and simmer for 5 minutes. Remove from heat and puree until smooth with an immersion blender.

• Reduce oven heat to 350°F. Spread a thin layer of sauce in the bottoms of 2 square baking dishes. Spoon 1/4 cup filling and 1 tablespoon of each cheese into a tortilla and roll up. Place the tortilla seam side down in the baking dish. Repeat with the remaining tortillas, laying each rolled tortilla snug against the others. Pour the remaining sauce evenly over the top. Sprinkle the remaining cheese on top (see photos, opposite page).

• Cover with foil and bake for 25 minutes. Serve warm.

*notes*

**Omit or substitute the cheese** to create a vegan dish.

**Use sprouted grain corn tortillas,** if you can find them, for an extra boost of nutrients. See sprouted grain info in our Ingredients section (page 18).

**You can roast the vegetables and make the sauce** one day in advance; store covered in the refrigerator.

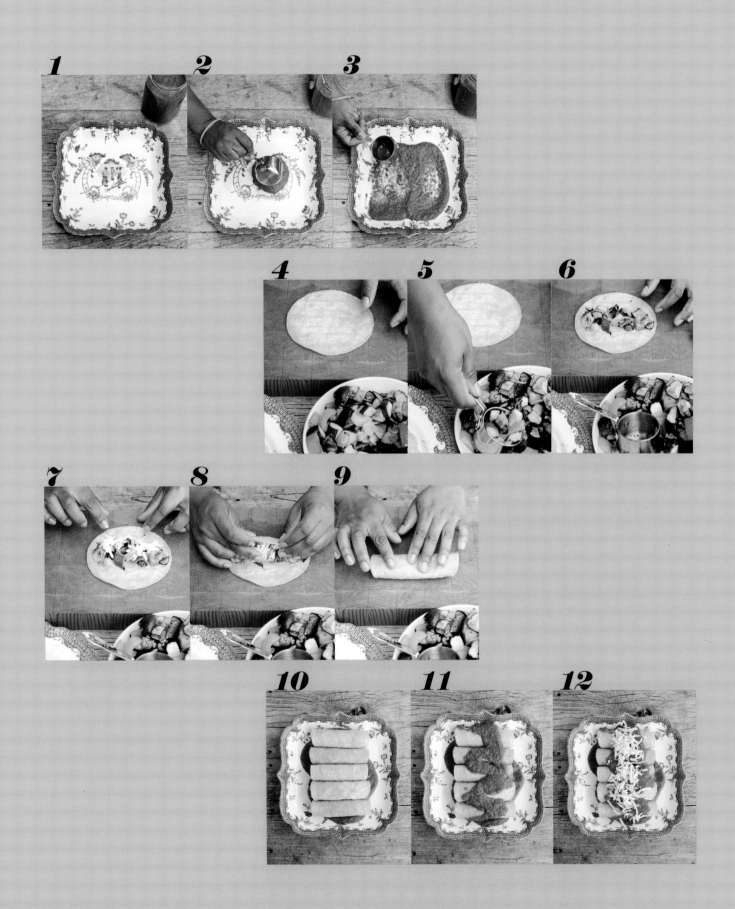

TOTAL TIME: 20 MINUTES PLUS FREEZING / MAKES ABOUT NINE 3-OUNCE POPS

# *horchata pops*

*5 tablespoons turbinado or raw sugar*

*5 tablespoons water*

*3 cups plain rice milk*

*1/2 teaspoon pure vanilla extract*

*1/4 teaspoon ground cinnamon*

*2 tablespoons cornstarch*

• In a small saucepan over medium heat, stir the water and sugar together until the sugar is melted.

• In a large saucepan, whisk together the rice milk, vanilla, cinnamon, and cornstarch.

• Pour the sugar syrup into the rice milk mixture. Bring to a boil while whisking gently. Let the mixture simmer for 2 minutes and then remove from heat.

• Cool the mixture down to room temperature or cooler before pouring into your ice pop molds. Freeze until solid, about 2 1/2 hours, and serve.

## *notes*

***These pops can be made*** in advance. They'll stay vibrant in the freezer for about a week.

***If you don't have ice pop molds,*** use freezer-proof cups (such as ramekins) covered in plastic wrap. Serve with spoons for scraping the ice milk.

# menu

|  | SPEEDY | MAKE AHEAD | VEGAN | VEGAN FLEX |
|---|---|---|---|---|
| *arugula + mozzarella salad with eggplant caponata* | | MA | | VF |
| *mediterranean roasted pork loin* | | MA | | |
| *roasted sweet potatoes with pistachios* | | MA | V | |
| *almond cookies with cherries + cream* | S | MA | | |

### WINE PAIRING

The sun-drenched vineyards of Sicily are great for Nero d'Avola and Nerello Mascalese, local grapes whose juicy wines sing with Mediterranean menus like this one. Producers to look for include Colosi, Ceuso, and Terre Nere, all of which produce terrific wines at lower price points.

### COOKING ORDER

*1.* cookies

*2.* potatoes

*3.* salad

*4.* pork loin

### WARDROBE CHANGE

Take the pork out of oven and let it rest while you change. Assemble the salad when guests arrive.

TOTAL TIME: 1 HOUR / SERVES 10

# arugula + mozzarella *salad*
## with eggplant caponata

**FOR THE CAPONATA:**

1 large eggplant, diced into 1/2-inch chunks

4 tablespoons extra virgin olive oil

2 tablespoons pine nuts

2 shallots, chopped

1 teaspoon red chile pepper flakes

2 Roma tomatoes, chopped

2 teaspoons turbinado or raw sugar

2 tablespoons dried currants

3 tablespoons red wine vinegar

1/2 cup tomato puree

1/2 teaspoon fine grain sea salt

1/4 teaspoon freshly ground black pepper

2 tablespoons fresh mint leaves cut into a chiffonade

2 tablespoons fresh basil leaves cut into a chiffonade

**FOR THE SALAD:**

6 cups baby arugula

2 tablespoons fine extra virgin olive oil

Fine grain sea salt and freshly ground black pepper

1 pound fresh mozzarella, cut into 1/2-inch cubes

• MAKE THE CAPONATA: Preheat the oven to 375°F. Toss the eggplant in 2 tablespoons olive oil and spread in an even layer on a rimmed baking sheet. Roast for 20 to 30 minutes, until cooked, stirring halfway through.

• Toast the pine nuts for 5 minutes on a rimmed baking sheet in the oven (you can do this while you roast the eggplant).

• In a medium pan, sauté the shallots over medium heat in 1 tablespoon olive oil until soft and starting to brown, 8 to 10 minutes. Add the chile flakes, tomatoes, sugar, currants, vinegar, tomato puree, salt, and pepper. Cook for an additional 5 minutes. Add the eggplant, then stir in the pine nuts, mint, basil, and remaining 1 tablespoon olive oil. Remove from heat and let cool to room temperature.

• MAKE THE SALAD: In a mixing bowl, toss the arugula with the fine olive oil and season with salt and pepper. Mix in the mozzarella.

• To serve, mound the caponata in the center of a platter. Sprinkle the dressed arugula and mozzarella around the caponata.

## *notes*

*Don't know how to make a chiffonade?* See Quick Reference (page 256).

*Served with crusty bread,* this also makes a great main-dish salad. Or, skip the salad and just serve the caponata with bread if you feel like that's enough food.

*The caponata can be made* one day in advance; store covered in the refrigerator.

*For a vegan dish,* omit the mozzarella.

# *mediterranean roasted* pork loin

1/4 cup dried currants

1/4 cup white wine, warmed

1 Vidalia onion, diced

1 tablespoon plus 1 teaspoon extra virgin olive oil

2 cloves garlic, minced

2 teaspoons grated lemon zest

1/4 cup chopped fresh flat-leaf parsley

1 tablespoon chopped fresh rosemary

1 tablespoon chopped fresh mint leaves

1/2 teaspoon fine grain sea salt, plus more for pork

1/4 teaspoon freshly ground black pepper, plus more for pork

1 (3-pound) boneless pork loin, butterflied

Olive oil cooking spray

• Preheat the oven to 350°F. In a small bowl, soak the currants in warm white wine.

• In a sauté pan over medium heat, sauté the onion with 1 teaspoon olive oil until it starts to brown, about 7 minutes. Remove from heat.

• Stir in the garlic, lemon zest, parsley, rosemary, and mint. Then stir in the currant-wine mixture, 1/2 teaspoon salt, and 1/4 teaspoon pepper.

• Spread the stuffing mixture evenly over the inside of the pork. Roll the pork back up and tie with kitchen twine. Rub the outside with 1 tablespoon olive oil. Season the outside with a sprinkle of salt and pepper.

• Place a large sauté pan over high heat and spray with olive oil. Sear the pork until all sides are browned, about 5 minutes.

• Place the meat on a rimmed baking sheet or 9x13-inch baking dish and roast in the oven for 30 minutes or until the meat reaches an internal temperature of 150°F. Tent the meat with foil and let rest for 20 minutes.

• Slice the meat as you remove the twine. Serve the pork arranged on a platter or individually plated, a few slices per plate.

**notes**

**You can ask the butcher** to butterfly the pork for you. To do it yourself, see Quick Reference (page 255).

**The filling** can be made one day in advance; store covered in the refrigerator.

TOTAL TIME: 45 MINUTES / SERVES 6 TO 8

MA V

# roasted sweet potatoes
## with pistachios

3 pounds sweet potatoes, peeled

4 tablespoons extra virgin olive oil

1/2 teaspoon fine grain sea salt

3/4 cup shelled, lightly crushed, raw pistachios

1/3 cup chopped fresh flat-leaf parsley

• Preheat the oven to 400°F. Line a rimmed baking sheet with parchment paper. Cut the sweet potatoes into 3/4-inch cubes and toss with 1 tablespoon olive oil and the salt. Spread them out on the prepared baking sheet and roast until fork tender, about 30 minutes, stirring occasionally.

• Place a sauté pan over low heat and add 3 tablespoons olive oil. When the oil is hot, add the pistachios and stir until toasty, about 5 minutes.

• In a large serving bowl, combine the pistachios and olive oil with the potatoes. Toss with the parsley and serve warm.

### notes

*The pistachio oil* can be made up to two days in advance; store in the refrigerator in a sealed conatiner.

TOTAL TIME: 1 HOUR, 30 MINUTES INCLUDING MARINATING / MAKES 40 BITE-SIZE COOKIES

# almond cookies
## *with cherries + cream*

*2 cups sweet cherries, pitted and halved*

*1 tablespoon kirsch*

*2/3 cup plus 1/4 cup turbinado or raw sugar*

*2 1/4 cups slivered almonds*

*2 egg whites*

*2 tablespoons water*

*1/8 teaspoon almond extract (optional)*

*1 cup cold whipping cream*

• In a bowl, mix together the cherries, kirsch, and 1/4 cup sugar. Let sit for 1 hour at room temperature.

• Preheat the oven to 325°F. Line a cookie sheet with parchment paper. Blend the almonds in a food processor until fine. Add 2/3 cup sugar, the egg whites, water, and almond extract (if using) and continue to blend until smooth. The dough will be sticky but fairly firm.

• Drop teaspoonfuls of batter onto the lined cookie sheet, leaving 1 inch of space between the cookies. Bake until the exteriors of the cookies are firm and most of the moisture is gone, about 12 minutes. Remove the cookies with a spatula to a cooling rack.

• Whip the cream with an electric mixer or whisk until firm peaks form; do not over whip.

• To serve, arrange the cookies on a platter with the cherries and whipped cream in separate serving bowls.

### notes

***The smoother you process your almonds,*** the smoother the cookies will be.

***See Quick Reference*** for detailed instructions on whipping cream (page 263).

***Encourage guests*** to grab a small plate with all the fixings and dip the cookies in the cherries and cream. Don't be afraid to get messy!

***These cookies tend to absorb moisture*** from the air; keep this in mind if you plan to make them a day in advance, as they can go from crispy to chewy. Store them in an airtight container.

***The cherries*** can be made one day in advance; keep refrigerated until ready to serve.

# menu

*anytime*

| | SPEEDY | MAKE AHEAD | VEGAN | VEGAN FLEX |
|---|---|---|---|---|
| *crab fritters with creamy mustard sauce* | | MA | | |
| *black-eyed peas* | | | | VF |
| *cider-braised collards* | | MA | V | |
| *baked peaches with gingersnap crumble* | | MA | | VF |

| WINE PAIRING | COOKING ORDER | WARDROBE CHANGE |
|---|---|---|
| Apple-scented Chardonnay is a safe bet with this combination, but make sure to choose one that emphasizes fruit over oak; even better if the wine was raised in stainless steel. Some of our favorite bargain Chards include Long Island's Shinn Estate and California's Calera. | **1.** collards<br>**2.** peas<br>**3.** fritters<br>**4.** crumble | Prep everything to completion except the crumble. Change. Put the crumble in the oven when guests arrive. If you're pressed for time, fry the fritters after your wardrobe change, and invite guests into the kitchen with you. |

TOTAL TIME: 30 MINUTES / MAKES ABOUT 15 FRITTERS

# crab fritters
## with creamy mustard sauce

**SAUCE:**

1/2 cup mayonnaise

1/4 cup finely chopped gherkins

1/2 teaspoon paprika

1 teaspoon Dijon mustard

2 tablespoons white wine vinegar

**FRITTERS:**

1/2 cup whole wheat pastry flour

1/4 cup cornmeal

1/2 teaspoon baking powder

1/2 teaspoon fine grain sea salt

1/4 teaspoon freshly ground black pepper

1 large egg

1/3 cup milk

8 ounces lump crab, picked through for shells

1 jalapeño pepper, seeds and ribs removed, diced small

4 scallions, chopped

1 ear corn, kernels sliced from cob

Vegetable oil, for frying

• MAKE THE SAUCE: In a bowl, mix together the mayonnaise, gherkins, paprika, Dijon, and vinegar. Store covered in the refrigerator until ready to serve.

• MAKE THE FRITTERS: Stir together the flour, cornmeal, baking powder, salt, and pepper.

• In a separate large bowl, stir together the egg and milk. Mix in the dry ingredients. Gently stir in the crab, jalapeño, scallions, and corn kernels.

• Line a plate with a paper towel. Heat 1/4 inch vegetable oil in a sauté pan over medium-low heat. Test the temperature of the oil with a piece of bread (see Quick Reference, page 262). Drop spoonfuls of batter into pan, being careful not to overcrowd the pan and fry until edges bubble, about 2 minutes. Flip. Cook another 2 minutes. Remove the finished fritters to the plate, letting the paper towel soak up excess oil. Continue cooking the fritters until all the batter is used. Serve with the sauce on the side.

*notes*

**The mustard sauce** can be made one day in advance; store covered in the refrigerator.

TOTAL TIME: 45 MINUTES / SERVES 6

**VF**

# black-eyed peas

*3 slices bacon, chopped*

*1/4 teaspoon smoked paprika*

*1/4 teaspoon cayenne pepper*

*2 cups cooked black-eyed peas*

*3/4 cup vegetable broth*

*2/3 cup diced red bell pepper*

*1/3 cup diced carrot*

*2 scallions, chopped*

*2 cloves garlic, minced*

*1/2 teaspoon fresh thyme leaves*

*1 teaspoon fine grain sea salt*

• Place the bacon in a medium sauté pan and turn the heat to medium-low; cook until crispy, about 10 minutes, turning occasionally. Add the paprika and cayenne and sauté for 1 minute.

• Add the black-eyed peas and vegetable broth. Bring to a simmer and add the remaining vegetables, garlic, thyme leaves, and salt. Cook until the vegetables are soft, about 10 more minutes.

## notes

**Using frozen black-eyed peas** saves time—no need to boil, just defrost! To cook your own from scratch, see Quick Reference (page 257).

**Omit the bacon** for a vegan dish. Add 1 tablespoon olive oil to the pan before adding the paprika and cayenne pepper.

---

TOTAL TIME: 40 MINUTES / SERVES 9

**MA** **V**

# cider-braised collards

*3 bunches collard greens (about 3 pounds), ribs removed, cut into 1-inch squares*

*1 quart apple cider*

*1 1/2 cups vegetable stock*

*1/2 teaspoon fine grain sea salt*

*Pinch of cayenne pepper*

• Place all the ingredients in a large pot. Simmer for 30 minutes over medium heat, uncovered, stirring occasionally. The collards will be dark green and tender when done. Adjust salt to taste.

## notes

**When purchasing collard greens,** look for leaves that are dark green not yellowing at the edges.

**Can be made** one day in advance. Store the greens in their liquid in a sealed container in the refrigerator. Reheat in a saucepan over medium heat until simmering.

TOTAL TIME: 60 MINUTES / SERVES 10

# baked peaches
## with gingersnap crumble

7 large ripe peaches, pitted and sliced

3 tablespoons fresh lime juice (from about 2 limes)

1 tablespoon grated fresh ginger

1/2 cup turbinado or raw sugar

8 ounces gingersnap cookies

1/4 cup brown sugar

4 tablespoons (1/2 stick) unsalted butter, cold

• Preheat the oven to 350°F. Toss the peaches with the lime juice, ginger, and sugar. Spread evenly in a 9x13-inch baking dish.

• Crumble the cookies with the brown sugar and butter in a food processor; process until the cookies are mostly broken up but some chunks remain. Sprinkle evenly over the peaches.

• Bake until peaches are bubbly and soft, about 40 minutes.

### notes

*Frozen peaches are fine* if making this dessert when peaches aren't in season. No need to defrost!

*When purchasing store-bought foods* like gingersnap cookies, remember to buy organic, whole grain versions. Whole grain gingersnaps are now available in many stores. Try to find the ones with the most recognizable, natural ingredients.

*You can make this one day in advance;* store covered in the refrigerator. Serve it warm by heating in a 350°F oven until hot.

*For a vegan dessert,* make sure your gingersnaps are vegan, and substitute the butter with 1 tablespoon coconut oil.

# menu

|  | SPEEDY | MAKE AHEAD | VEGAN | VEGAN FLEX |
|---|---|---|---|---|
| *avocado toasts* | S | MA | V | |
| *cheese + tofu quesadillas* | | | | VF |
| *chipotle sweet potato salad* | | MA | V | |
| *green chile–glazed pineapple* | S | MA | | |

| WINE PAIRING | COOKING ORDER | WARDROBE CHANGE |
|---|---|---|
| A cold lager like Negra Modelo works well here, as do Champagne-style Crémants from Jura, Alsace, and Bourgogne. | *1.* salad<br>*2.* quesadillas<br>*3.* toasts<br>*4.* pineapple | Prep everything, make the salad and the quesadillas, change, and then spread the avocado on your toast and remove the dessert from the oven. |

TOTAL TIME: 20 MINUTES / SERVES 10

# *avocado toasts*

10 slices whole grain bread

Olive oil cooking spray

1/4 teaspoon fine grain sea salt

3 ripe Hass avocados

2 tablespoons fresh lemon juice
(from about 1 lemon)

1 teaspoon red chile pepper
flakes

• Preheat the oven to 425°F. Line a cookie sheet with parchment paper. Lay the bread slices flat on the cookie sheet, not overlapping. Spray with a little olive oil and dust lightly with salt. Toast the bread slices on one side in the oven until golden brown, about 5 minutes. Cut in half diagonally. Set aside.

• Mash the avocados with lemon juice and 1/2 teaspoon red pepper flakes. Spread over toasted bread. Sprinkle the remaining pepper flakes on top.

*notes*

*You can make the spread and toasts 15 to 20 minutes before guests arrive,* just cover and refrigerate the avocado spread. Apply the spread as guests start to trickle in. This will prevent browned avocado (yuck).

*Add grilled shrimp to make a simple lunch.* Jill does a version of this almost every day when she's on the West Coast.

TOTAL TIME: 60 MINUTES / SERVES 8

VF

# cheese + tofu quesadillas

1 pound soft tofu (about 1 package), drained

1 tablespoon dried oregano

1/2 clove garlic, minced

2 tablespoons chopped fresh cilantro, plus a little for garnish

2 tablespoons chopped jalapeño pepper, seeds and ribs removed

1/4 teaspoon fine grain sea salt

1 tablespoon extra virgin olive oil

Olive oil cooking spray

2 cups shredded mozzarella

2 cups shredded Monterey jack cheese

8 large sprouted-grain tortillas

• Preheat the oven to 325°F. In a bowl, combine the tofu, oregano, garlic, cilantro, jalapeño, salt, and olive oil.

• Spray a sauté pan with olive oil and place over medium heat; add the tofu mixture and sauté, breaking up the tofu like scrambled eggs, for 10 minutes or until fragrant.

• Spread half of each tortilla with some of the tofu mixture and top evenly with the cheeses. Fold tortillas in half over the filling.

• Spray a clean sauté pan with olive oil and toast quesadillas on both sides until cheese is melted. Place quesadillas on a cookie sheet, cover with foil, and place in the oven to keep warm as you cook the rest.

• Garnish each tortilla with a sprinkle of cilantro. Slice each into quarters and serve hot.

**notes**

**For a vegan dish,** use vegan cheese or omit the cheese altogether.

TOTAL TIME: 45 MINUTES / SERVES 10

MA V

# chipotle sweet potato *salad*

4 sweet potatoes, diced medium
(about 5 cups)

1/4 cup plus 1 tablespoon extra
virgin olive oil

3/4 teaspoon fine grain sea salt

**DRESSING:**

1 chipotle pepper from a can

1 tablespoon adobo sauce from
chipotle can

2 tablespoons fresh lime juice
(from about 2 limes)

1/4 cup chopped fresh cilantro

1 clove garlic

1/2 teaspoon ground cumin

1/4 teaspoon freshly ground
black pepper

2 heads romaine lettuce,
chopped

• Preheat the oven to 425°F. Toss the sweet potatoes
with 1 tablespoon olive oil and 1/2 teaspoon salt. Spread
out on a rimmed baking sheet and roast for 25 minutes
or until fork tender, stirring after 15 minutes. Let cool.

• MAKE THE DRESSING: Blend the chipotle pepper,
adobo sauce, lime juice, cilantro, garlic, cumin, 1/4
teaspoon salt, pepper, and 1/4 cup olive oil in a
blender.

• Toss the lettuce and sweet potatoes
with the dressing.

## *notes*

**The dressing can be made**
one day in advance; store
covered in the refrigerator.
You can also roast the sweet
potatoes one day in advance
and store covered in the
refrigerator. Toss everything
together just before serving.

TOTAL TIME: 1 HOUR / SERVES 10

S MA

# green chile–glazed *pineapple*

1 ripe pineapple, peeled and cored (see Note)

1/2 cup honey

1/4 teaspoon fine grain sea salt

1/2 green chile pepper, such as jalapeño, seeded and minced

1 teaspoon unsalted butter

1/4 cup crème fraîche

2 tablespoons confectioners' sugar

• Preheat the oven to 325°F. Line a rimmed baking sheet with parchment paper. Slice the pineapple into 1/2-inch rings. Arrange pineapple rings (or slices if you don't have a corer) on the lined baking sheet.

• In a small saucepan over medium heat, combine the honey, salt, green chile, and butter. Bring to a boil then remove from heat. Cover and let steep for 5 minutes.

• Drizzle the chile-honey over the pineapple with reckless abandon. Bake until browned, about 35 minutes.

• Meanwhile, mix the crème fraîche with confectioners' sugar. Let the pineapple cool for 5 to 10 minutes and serve with crème fraîche on the side.

*notes*

**If you don't have a pineapple corer,** just leave the core in and slice into rounds.

**The crème fraîche can be made** one day in advance, as can the honey chile sauce; store both covered in the refrigerator. Reheat the sauce before drizzling over the pineapple. Don't bake the pineapple until shortly before serving. The warm pineapple juice is worth the extra balancing act.

# menu

| | SPEEDY | MAKE AHEAD | VEGAN | VEGAN FLEX |
|---|---|---|---|---|
| **roasted garlic** | | MA | V | |
| **skirt steak with quick pickled leeks, scapes + gigante beans** | | MA | | |
| **smoky kale + chickpeas** | | | V | |
| **strawberry cornmeal cake** | | MA | | |

| WINE PAIRING | COOKING ORDER | WARDROBE CHANGE |
|---|---|---|
| Spanish Rioja comes in a variety of styles, all of which work well with the elements in this savory repast. If you like your wines bold and juicy, wines labeled as crianza, reservas, and gran reservas boast supple flavors and silken texture. Muga, Lopez de Heredia, and Cvne produce delicious examples of each. | *1.* steak<br>*2.* cake<br>*3.* garlic<br>*4.* kale | Do everything except sear the steaks before you change. Put on an apron before handling the meat! |

TOTAL TIME: 55 MINUTES / SERVES 8

MA V

# *roasted garlic*

4 heads garlic

Extra virgin olive oil

Coarse salt and freshly ground
black pepper

Fresh herbs, such as thyme,
rosemary, or oregano

Crusty French bread, grilled
(see Quick Reference, page
262)

• Preheat the oven to 400°F. Slice off the pointy tops of
the garlic heads (not the root ends). Place each on a
separate piece of aluminum foil, cut side up, and drizzle
with olive oil, a little salt and pepper, and a sprig of any
herb you have lying around.

• Wrap the foil around each head
of garlic and place them on a
cookie sheet; roast for 45 minutes
to 1 hour. Let cool slightly and
press the whole cloves out of their shell or serve in their shell. Serve
warm with grilled bread and let guests smooth the garlic over the toasts
with a butter knife.

## notes

*If making this menu in full,*
roast an extra head of garlic for
the kale and chickpeas (page 78).

*The garlic* can be roasted one
day in advance. Leave them in
their shells and foil. Rewarm in
the oven so the cloves slip out
easily.

*Roasted garlic* can be used in
place of raw garlic in almost any
dish to add depth of flavor. If you
have time for the extra step, do it!

TOTAL TIME: ABOUT 6 HOURS INCLUDING MARINATING, BEAN COOKING + PICKLING / SERVES 10

--------------------------------------------------------------------------------

# *skirt steak* with quick pickled leeks, scapes + gigante beans

3/4 cup dried gigante beans, soaked overnight

1 1/2 cups water

1/2 cup white wine vinegar

3/4 cup turbinado or raw sugar

2 bay leaves

5 juniper berries

5 garlic scapes, sliced into 2-inch spears

2 leeks, rinsed and sliced into 1/4-inch rounds

3 pounds skirt steak

2/3 cup red wine

2 tablespoons extra virgin olive oil

Olive oil cooking spray

Fine grain sea salt and freshly ground black pepper

• Simmer the beans in a large pot of unsalted water until fork-tender but not mushy, 3 hours. Drain and let cool.

• To make the pickling juice, boil 1 1/2 cups water, the vinegar, sugar, bay leaves, and juniper berries for 5 minutes in a large nonreactive pot. Let cool to room temperature.

• Arrange the beans, scapes, and leeks in a large glass container. Pour the pickling liquid over the vegetables and let sit, covered, for 2 or more hours. Be sure the vegetables are fully immersed in the liquid; add more water if needed.

• Place the steak, red wine, and olive oil in a closed container or sealed plastic bag and place in the refrigerator to marinate, 2 to 3 hours.

• Remove the steak from the marinade and pat dry. Spray a large, heavy-bottom sauté pan with olive oil spray and heat the pan over medium-high heat. Sear the steaks until browned on both sides, 5 minutes per side for medium, working in batches, if necessary. Alternatively, you can grill or broil the steak. Let the steak rest for 5 minutes, then slice against the grain. Sprinkle with salt and pepper to taste. Ladle pickled vegetables over the steak and serve.

*notes*

*Juniper berries,* which have the clear flavor of a good gin, are found in the spice aisle of your grocery.

*Other white beans* work well with this recipe, like cannellini, northern white beans, or even lima beans (yeah, they're green).

*See Quick Reference* for more info on cutting leeks (page 260) and cooking beans (page 257).

*The pickles can be made* two to three days in advance; store in an airtight container in the refrigerator.

*If there are extra,* the pickles make a great snack, even days after the party.

TOTAL TIME: 1 HOUR, 15 MINUTES / SERVES 6

# smoky kale + chickpeas

1 head garlic, roasted (see page 75)

1 tablespoon plus 1 teaspoon extra virgin olive oil

1 onion, sliced thinly

3 cups cooked chickpeas

1/2 teaspoon smoked paprika

2 bunches kale (about 2 pounds), ribs removed, chopped

1 cup water

1/2 teaspoon fine grain sea salt

1/4 teaspoon freshly ground black pepper

• Place a sauté pan over low heat. Heat 1 tablespoon olive oil in the pan, then add the onions. Sauté them, stirring occasionally, until deep golden brown and caramelized, 20 to 30 minutes. Add the chickpeas and paprika. Continue to cook for 5 minutes. Add the kale and 1 cup water. Season with salt and pepper and cook, uncovered, for 20 minutes.

• Squeeze the roasted cloves of garlic from their shell and toss them with the kale just before plating. Serve warm.

## notes

See Quick Reference (page 257) for tips on cooking chickpeas.

The garlic can be roasted one day in advance. Leave it in the shell and the foil. Rewarm in the oven so that the cloves slip out easily.

People love this dish because it tastes of smoky pork, thanks to the paprika. Remember that a little smoked paprika goes a long way; it's easy to go overboard.

TOTAL TIME: 1 HOUR, 30 MINUTES / SERVES 10

- - - - - - - - - - - - - - - - - - - - - - - - - - - - - - - - - - - - - - - - - - - - **MA**

# strawberry cornmeal *cake*

**BERRIES:**

*1/2 cup turbinado or raw sugar*

*4 tablespoons (1/2 stick) unsalted butter*

*1/2 vanilla bean*

*1 pint strawberries, hulled and sliced in half*

**CAKE:**

*1 cup whole wheat pastry flour*

*1/2 cup coarse cornmeal*

*2 teaspoons baking powder*

*1/4 teaspoon fine grain sea salt*

*3/4 cup turbinado or raw sugar*

*2 large eggs*

*1/2 vanilla bean*

*1/2 cup milk*

• Preheat the oven to 350°F.

• PREPARE THE BERRIES: Dissolve the sugar and butter in a saucepan over medium heat until the mixture browns a little. Scrape the seeds of the vanilla bean into the mixture and stir.

• Pour the butter-sugar mixture into the bottom of a 8-inch square cake pan. Spread the strawberries on top of the mixture, reserving a few to garnish the cake.

• MAKE THE CAKE: Combine the flour, cornmeal, baking powder, and salt in a large bowl.

• In another bowl, mix together the sugar, eggs, seeds from the vanilla bean, and the milk. Add mixture to the dry ingredients and stir gently until just combined.

• Pour the batter over the strawberries and bake until a toothpick inserted into the cake comes out clean, about 50 minutes.

• Top with a few berries for garnish and serve from the pan.

## notes

*For more info on how to use vanilla beans,* see Quick Reference (page 263).

*This can be made in advance,* but it's best served warm from the oven.

*When making this dish,* prepare to watch your guests lose control. We've seen them scraping the bits from the side of the pan!

anytime

# *menu*

|  | SPEEDY | MAKE AHEAD | VEGAN | VEGAN FLEX |
|---|---|---|---|---|
| *spiced roasted chickpeas* | | MA | V | |
| *balsamic-marinated salmon* | | MA | | |
| *cayenne-flecked corn pudding* | | MA | | |
| *cherry watermelon granita* | | MA | V | |

## WINE PAIRING

While we approve of any and all bubbles for breakfast, lunch, and dinner, calling for Champagne warrants a proper one; it's hard to beat an opulent Blanc de Noirs (white wine from red grapes, in this case Pinot Noir grapes) Champagne. For those who prefer red, a cherry-scented Oregon Pinot Noir would also be a worthy companion here.

## COOKING ORDER

*1.* granita

*2.* chickpeas

*3.* corn pudding

*4.* salmon

## WARDROBE CHANGE

Make everything, put the fish in oven, and change. Since each dish can at least be made partially ahead, you should have plenty of time for a full grooming and dress-up session.

TOTAL TIME: 1 HOUR, 15 MINUTES / SERVES 10

# spiced roasted *chickpeas*

5 cups cooked chickpeas, rinsed
and patted dry

3 tablespoons Chili Pop
(page 245)

3 tablespoons extra virgin olive
oil

• Preheat the oven to 400°F. Line a rimmed baking sheet with aluminum foil. Mix all ingredients in a bowl, coating the chickpeas. Spread the chickpeas evenly on the prepared baking sheet.

• Bake until crisp, stirring occasionally, about 1 hour.

• Let cool while spread out on pan. They will crisp more as they cool. Serve at room temp as a snack.

## *notes*

**See Quick Reference** (page 257) for tips on how to cook chickpeas.

**You MUST let the spiced chickpeas cool on the tray—** they keep crisping up. If you pour them into a bowl while hot, they get soggy. Patience, grasshopper.

**This can be made** one day in advance; store in an airtight container in a cool, dry place.

TOTAL TIME: 1 HOUR, 20 MINUTES INCLUDING MARINATING / SERVES 10

MA

# balsamic-marinated *salmon*

1 1/2 cups balsamic vinegar

4 cloves garlic, smashed

3 tablespoons extra virgin olive oil

1 tablespoon grated lemon zest

5 tablespoons fresh basil leaves cut into a chiffonade, loosely packed

1/2 teaspoon fine grain sea salt

1/4 teaspoon freshly ground black pepper

3 pounds salmon fillet

• Place a small nonreactive saucepan over low heat and add the balsamic vinegar and garlic. Cook to reduce by half, 15 to 20 minutes. Remove from heat and let cool to room temperature.

• MAKE THE MARINADE: Whisk together the vinegar reduction, olive oil, lemon zest, basil, salt, and pepper.

• Place the salmon in a baking dish and add the marinade. Marinate the salmon, covered, for 30 minutes in the refrigerator.

• Preheat the oven to 400°F. Line a rimmed baking sheet with parchment paper. Remove the salmon from the marinade and place it on the lined cookie sheet. Roast the salmon in oven until it flakes easily, about 15 minutes.

## notes

**Don't know how to make a chiffonade?** See Quick Reference (page 256).

**Marinade can be made** one day in advance; store covered in the refrigerator.

**This is also a great marinade** for other meats and even some vegetables. See the grill guide for suggestions (pages 230–233).

TOTAL TIME: 1 HOUR, 30 MINUTES / SERVES 10

MA

# cayenne-flecked *corn pudding*

4 cups fresh corn kernels (from about 6 ears)

4 large eggs, lightly beaten

1/4 cup cornmeal

1 cup milk

2 tablespoons unsalted butter, melted

2 tablespoons turbinado or raw sugar

1/2 teaspoon fine grain sea salt

1/4 teaspoon cayenne pepper, plus more for garnish

Olive oil cooking spray

• Preheat the oven to 350°F. Blend half the corn in a food processor until fairly smooth.

• In a bowl, mix all of the corn with the eggs, cornmeal, milk, butter, sugar, salt, and cayenne.

• Spray a 10 x 10-inch baking dish with olive oil and pour in the batter. Dust with a little more cayenne. Bake, uncovered, until liquid is no longer runny, about 1 hour.

## notes

*You can shave the corn* one day in advance (see Quick Reference, page 258). Store refrigerated in an airtight plastic bag so it doesn't dry out.

TOTAL TIME: 15 MINUTES PLUS FREEZING / SERVES 10

MA V

# cherry watermelon *granita*

9 cups diced seedless
watermelon

1/4 cup fresh lime juice (from
about 4 limes)

1/4 cup turbinado or raw sugar

3 sprigs fresh rosemary,
stemmed

2 cups pitted and halved sweet
cherries

• Working in batches, blend the watermelon, lime juice, sugar, and rosemary in a blender until smooth. Stir in the cherries.

• Freeze in a covered container until hard, stirring occasionally, about 3 to 4 hours.

• To serve, remove from freezer and let it sit out at room temperature for 5 minutes. Use a spoon to scrape the watermelon ice into serving glasses.

## notes

**This can be made** one day in advance; keep frozen.

**Stir the mixture occasionally as it freezes** to be sure the cherries don't all sink to the bottom. We have made that same silly mistake.

anytime

# *menu*

| | SPEEDY | MAKE AHEAD | VEGAN | VEGAN FLEX |
|---|---|---|---|---|
| **caramelized-onion crème fraîche with blistered veggies** | |  | | |
| **miso caper glazed salmon** | | | |  |
| **warm squash salad with farro, hazelnuts + currants** | |  |  | |
| **maple cream cheese cookie sandwiches** | |  | | |

## WINE PAIRING

Enticingly floral Alsatian Muscat tackles the salmon and tangy components in this menu with a grace and poise that you're sure to abandon after one sip. If you can't find an Alsatian Muscat, Austria and northern Italy produce equally delicious examples. A salmon-hued rosé from the Côtes de Provence or a hot pink pour from the Loire Valley will also provide plenty of pleasure.

## COOKING ORDER

*1.* cookies
*2.* salad
*3.* crème fraîche
*4.* salmon

## WARDROBE CHANGE

Make everything, pop the fish in oven, then change. Assembling the cookies lends itself well to doing with your friends.

TOTAL TIME: 60 MINUTES / SERVES 10

MA

# caramelized-onion *crème fraîche* with blistered veggies

3 teaspoons extra virgin olive oil

1 tablespoon unsalted butter

2 cups chopped sweet onion, such as Vidalia

1 1/4 teaspoons fine grain sea salt, plus more for blanching water

1/2 cup crème fraîche

1/2 cup nonfat yogurt

1/4 teaspoon freshly ground black pepper

4 cups trimmed, halved Brussels sprouts

4 carrots, peeled, trimmed, and chopped into 2-inch chunks

4 parsnips, peeled, trimmed, and chopped into 2-inch chunks

1 sweet potato, peeled, cut into 2- to 3-inch-long wedges

• Place a sauté pan over medium-low heat. Add 1 teaspoon olive oil, the butter, onions, and 1/2 teaspoon salt; cook until onions are tender and brown, about 25 minutes, stirring every 5 minutes or so. Remove from heat and let the onions cool to room temperature.

• Stir in the crème fraîche, yogurt, 1/2 teaspoon salt, and the pepper. Set aside in a small serving bowl.

• Place a pot of water over high heat to boil; add salt. Blanch the vegetables for about 2 minutes, then submerge in an ice bath. Drain well.

• Set a sauté pan over high heat and add the remaining 2 teaspoons olive oil. Sauté the blanched vegetables with 1/4 teaspoon salt until caramelized all around the outside, 8 to 10 minutes.

• Serve vegetables at room temperature with the onion crème fraîche as a dipping sauce.

## notes

**You can make the dip** one day in advance; store covered in the refrigerator.

**For more information on blanching,** see Quick Reference (page 255).

TOTAL TIME: 1 HOUR, 30 MINUTES INCLUDING MARINATING / SERVES 6 TO 8

VF

# *miso caper glazed* **salmon**

*1/4 cup capers packed in brine*

*1/4 cup white miso*

*1/4 cup extra virgin olive oil*

*2 tablespoons agave syrup*

*1/2 cup mirin*

*2 pounds salmon fillet*

• Crush the capers with a fork. Whisk together the capers, miso, olive oil, agave, and mirin.

• Slice the salmon fillet into 8 pieces and marinate the salmon with the miso-caper mixture in a covered dish or sealable plastic bag for 1 hour in the refrigerator.

• Preheat the oven to 425°F. Line a rimmed baking sheet with parchment paper. Place the salmon on the baking sheet and bake until salmon is opaque and flakes easily, about 20 minutes.

*notes*

**For a vegan dish,** substitute tempeh or portabello mushrooms for the fish.

TOTAL TIME: 60 MINUTES / SERVES 6 TO 8

MA V

# *warm squash salad*
## *with farro, hazelnuts + currants*

*1 1/2 pounds delicata or butternut squash, peeled (see Note)*

*1 tablespoon chopped fresh sage leaves*

*3 tablespoons honey*

*1 quart water*

*1/2 cup farro*

*1/2 teaspoon fine grain sea salt, plus more for farro water*

*1 tablespoon apple cider vinegar*

*1 tablespoon extra virgin olive oil*

*1 tablespoon minced shallot*

*1/4 cup dried currants*

*1/4 cup chopped fresh flat-leaf parsley*

*1/3 cup peeled hazelnuts, toasted and chopped lightly (see Quick Reference, page 259)*

• Preheat the oven to 375°F. Cut the squash in half lengthwise, remove the seeds, and cut the squash into slices 1/4-inch thick. Chop each slice in half to get chunks.

• Toss the squash with sage and 2 tablespoons honey. Spread out on a rimmed baking sheet and roast until the squash is fork tender, about 15 minutes. Let cool.

• Place the water, farro, and salt in a pot over medium heat; simmer, uncovered, until tender, about 35 minutes; drain. Let cool slightly.

• Mix together 1 tablespoon honey, the vinegar, olive oil, and shallot until thoroughly combined.

• In a large bowl, toss the farro with the dressing and currants. Add the parsley, squash, and hazelnuts and mix gently until combined. Serve at room temperature.

## notes

*Delicata* doesn't need peeling, other squashes do and may be harder to peel.

*If using butternut squash,* quarter it lengthwise and then continue with the recipe.

*Farro* is an ancient grain commonly used in the Mediterranean. If you cannot find it, barley makes a good substitute.

*Hazelnuts* are expensive, but here are a few other uses for the extras: in your chocolate chip cookies (page 223) or toasted and added to a salad (page 199).

*This salad can be made* one day in advance; store covered in the refrigerator.

TOTAL TIME: 45 MINUTES PLUS COOLING / MAKES ABOUT 15 COOKIE SANDWICHES

MA

## *maple cream cheese*
# cookie sandwiches

**COOKIES:**

*12 tablespoons (1 1/2 sticks) unsalted butter, at room temperature*

*2/3 cup turbinado or raw sugar*

*1/3 cup maple syrup*

*1 large egg*

*1 3/4 cups whole wheat pastry flour*

*1/4 teaspoon ground allspice*

*1 teaspoon ground cinnamon*

*1/4 teaspoon fine grain sea salt*

*1/2 teaspoon baking powder*

**CREAM CHEESE FILLING:**

*4 ounces cream cheese, at room temperature*

*4 tablespoons (1/2 stick) unsalted butter, at room temperature*

*1 1/4 cups confectioners' sugar*

*3/4 teaspoon pure vanilla extract*

• MAKE THE COOKIES: Preheat the oven to 350°F. Line a cookie sheet with parchment paper. Cream the butter, sugar, and maple syrup together in a large bowl with an electric mixer until fluffy, about 5 minutes. Beat the egg into the mixture until combined.

• In a medium bowl, combine the flour, allspice, cinnamon, salt, and baking powder. Add them to the butter mixture. Stir until just combined.

• Drop heaping teaspoons of the dough onto the lined cookie sheet about 1 inch apart. Bake until cookies are puffy and a toothpick inserted in the center comes out clean, 9 to 10 minutes.

• Remove cookies to a wire rack to cool.

• MAKE THE FILLING: With an electric mixer, whip the cream cheese and butter together until fluffy, about 5 minutes. Add the sugar and mix until smooth. Stir in the vanilla.

• Spread 1 to 2 teaspoons filling on the bottom sides of 15 cookies. Press another cookie on top, bottom side facing the filling.

## *notes*

**When making these** on a hot day, you should put them in the fridge to stay firm. Make them in advance and wrap them in plastic wrap; store in the refrigerator. Let them come to room temperature before serving.

**You can also serve** these as open-face frosted cookies.

# *menu*

| | SPEEDY | MAKE AHEAD | VEGAN | VEGAN FLEX |
|---|---|---|---|---|
| *watermelon black pepper salad* | | MA | | VF |
| *granola-crusted cod* | | | | VF |
| *orrechiette + green bean salad* | | MA | | VF |
| *cinnamon corn ice cream with blueberries* | | MA | | |
| *dream sequins* | | | V | |

| WINE PAIRING | COOKING ORDER | WARDROBE CHANGE |
|---|---|---|
| The Chenin Blanc–based white wines of the Loire Valley work surprisingly well with vegetable pastas and white fish. Look for demi-sec Vouvray, Montlouis, or Anjou blanc. Or, go straight for our Dream Sequins cocktail. | *1.* ice cream <br> *2.* pasta salad <br> *3.* watermelon salad <br> *4.* cod <br> *5.* cocktails | Do everything except adding the crust and baking the fish. Do these after you've changed and once the guests have started to arrive. The cocktails should be made to order throughout the party. |

TOTAL TIME: 45 MINUTES / SERVES 10

# *watermelon black pepper* **salad**

**DRESSING:**

*1 cup balsamic vinegar*

*1 1/2 tablespoons turbinado or raw sugar*

*Olive oil cooking spray*

*1/4 watermelon, cut into 1-inch slices, with rind (2 to 3 pounds)*

*1/2 pound baby arugula*

*1 bunch watercress (about 1 pound), thick stems removed*

*2 tablespoons fresh mint leaves cut into a chiffonade*

*1/4 pound feta, crumbled*

*1 1/2 teaspoons coarsely ground black pepper*

*Fine extra virgin olive oil, for drizzling*

*Fine grain sea salt*

• MAKE THE DRESSING: Combine the balsamic vinegar and sugar in a small nonreactive saucepan over low heat and cook until reduced and syrupy, about 20 minutes (you should have about 1/4 cup). Be careful not to burn it.

• Preheat a grill to medium-high heat. Carefully oil the grill with olive oil spray or an oil-moistened cloth. Grill the melon slices until browned, about 3 minutes per side, turning with tongs by holding the rind. Let cool.

• In a large bowl, mix together the arugula, watercress, and mint. Top with melon slices. Sprinkle with feta and black pepper. Drizzle with a fruity olive oil and the balsamic reduction. Guests can add salt to taste.

## *notes*

**Don't know how to make a chiffonade?** See Quick Reference (page 256).

**No grill or grill pan?** Try serving the watermelon raw.

**You can reduce the balsamic** one day in advance; store at room temperature in a sealed container.

**Omit the cheese** for a vegan dish.

TOTAL TIME: 1 HOUR, 10 MINUTES INCLDING MARINATING / SERVES 8

VF

# *granola-crusted cod*

2 tablespoons maple syrup

1/2 cup fresh orange juice
(from about 2 oranges)

3 tablespoons chopped dried
cranberries

2 1/2 pounds fresh cod

2 tablespoons unsalted butter

1/2 cup slivered almonds

3/4 cup rolled oats, coarsely
chopped in a food processor

1/2 teaspoon fine grain sea salt

• Preheat the oven to 400°F. Line a rimmed baking
sheet with parchment paper.

• MAKE THE MAPLE GLAZE: Whisk together the maple
syrup, orange juice, and cranberries.

• Slice the fish into 8 portions and place in a sealable
plastic bag or glass container with a lid. Set aside half
the glaze and pour the other half over the fish. Marinate
for 20 to 30 minutes in the refrigerator.

• Melt the butter in a sauté
pan over medium heat. Add
the almonds. Stir to toast for 2 minutes. Add the oats and salt and
continue to toast until all is golden brown. Remove from heat and let
cool slightly.

• Remove the fish from the marinade and place on lined baking
sheet. Pour the reserved marinade over the fish. Pat the granola on
top of the fish. Place in the oven and bake until the fish is opaque
and flakes easily, about 20 minutes.

## *notes*

**Substitute** tofu for fish and oil for
butter for a vegan dish.

***This dish was inspired by*** the aKa
Café in Manhattan's Lower East Side
in 2003. Jill was just in love with their
granola-crusted trout. "I barely
remember anything about their recipe
but I remember swooning!"

TOTAL TIME: 45 MINUTES / SERVES 8

MA VF

# orrechiette + green bean *salad*

2 yellow tomatoes, cut into wedges

1/4 cup plus 1 teaspoon extra virgin olive oil

1/2 teaspoon fine grain sea salt, plus more for pasta water

1/2 pound orrechiette pasta

1 pound haricots verts, trimmed

1 bunch red Swiss chard (about 1 pound), sliced on bias

1/2 cup white balsamic vinegar

1 tablespoon Dijon mustard

1 clove garlic, minced

1/4 teaspoon freshly ground black pepper

2 tablespoons fresh basil leaves cut into a chiffonade

8 ounces ricotta salata cheese, crumbled

• Preheat the oven to 400°F. Toss the tomatoes in 1 teaspoon olive oil. Spread out on a rimmed baking sheet and roast for 10 minutes. Remove from the oven and let cool.

• Place a pot of water over high heat to boil; add salt. Cook the pasta until al dente, about 8 minutes. Drain and let cool.

• Meanwhile, place another pot of water over high heat to boil; add salt. Blanch the beans until bright green, 30 seconds to 1 minute. Use tongs to remove beans from water and rinse under cold water.

• Blanch the chard in the same pot of salted water, 30 seconds. Drain and rinse under cold water. Lightly squeeze out excess water.

• To make the dressing, whisk together 1/4 cup olive oil, vinegar, Dijon, garlic, 1/2 teaspoon salt, and pepper.

• In a large salad bowl, toss the pasta and haricot verts with the dressing. Stir in the chard, basil, and cheese. Serve cold or at room temperature.

## notes

*If you can't find haricots verts*, standard green beans will work just fine.

*Don't know how to make a chiffonade?* See Quick Reference (page 256).

*You can use the same boiling water* to blanch all your vegetables but you need new water to boil your pasta; otherwise the pasta will be bitter.

*Make the salad one day in advance;* store covered in the refrigerator and add the cheese before serving.

*Omit the cheese* for a vegan dish.

TOTAL TIME: 45 MINUTES PLUS STEEPING + FREEZING / MAKES 1 QUART OF ICE CREAM, ABOUT 8 SERVINGS

# cinnamon corn ice cream
## with blueberries

4 ears corn, shucked

3 1/2 cups whole milk

2 cinnamon sticks

Pinch of fine grain sea salt

1/2 cup turbinado or raw sugar

1/5 vanilla bean, split and seeded

3 tablespoons cornstarch

Blueberries, for garnish

• Cut the kernels off the cob, reserving the cobs (see Quick Reference, page 258). Blend the kernels with 1 cup milk in a food processor until smooth.

• In a large pot over low heat, combine the corn-milk mixture, 2 cups milk, and the corn cobs. Bring to a simmer over low heat then add the cinnamon sticks, salt, sugar, and vanilla pod and seeds. Simmer for 20 minutes, uncovered. Remove from heat. For more flavor, let this mixture steep overnight in the refrigerator. With tongs, remove the cobs, vanilla pod, and cinnamon sticks.

• Mix together the remaining 1/2 cup milk with the cornstarch. Whisk it into the pot with corn-milk mixture and bring to a boil to thicken the mixture. Once it starts to boil, reduce the heat and let it simmer for 5 minutes, stirring gently. Remove from heat and let cool to room temperature.

• Follow instructions on your ice cream maker to freeze. Serve topped with fresh blueberries.

### notes

**Make this** up to one week in advance. Store in an airtight container in the freezer.

**If you don't have an ice cream maker,** make milkshakes! Omit the cornstarch and add 1 scoop of vanilla ice cream to 1/2 cup of the corn base and blend for each serving.

TOTAL TIME: 10 MINUTES / SERVES 6

# dream sequins

1 cup vodka, chilled

3 tablespoons agave syrup

6 cups hulled strawberries

2 teaspoons grated fresh ginger

10 fresh mint leaves

2 teaspoons fresh lemon juice
(from about 1 lemon)

12 large ice cubes (about 4
cups)

• Put everything in a blender.  Blend until smooth and
serve.

## notes

**Make this drink in batches,** to order, otherwise it will melt before it can be enjoyed.

# *menu* anytime

| | SPEEDY | MAKE AHEAD | VEGAN | VEGAN FLEX |
|---|---|---|---|---|
| *sweet pea guacamole* | S | MA | V | |
| *corn + tomato salad* | S | | V | |
| *collard-wrapped burritos* | | MA | | VF |
| *mexican goddess chocolate pudding* | S | | V | |

## WINE PAIRING

Refreshing Provence rosé or Garnacha-based rosado from the Navarra region of Spain are affordable and delicious with festive spreads like these, or simplify with a couple 6-packs of Pacifico beer.

## COOKING ORDER

1. guacamole
2. salad
3. pudding
4. burritos

## WARDROBE CHANGE

Finish all of your prep, change, then bake the burritos after guests arrive.

TOTAL TIME: 20 MINUTES / SERVES 10

S MA V

## *sweet pea* **guacamole**

2 pounds peas, fresh or frozen

2 teaspoons ground cumin

3 tablespoons fresh lime juice
from about 3 limes

2 teaspoons grated lime zest

1 1/2 teaspoons fine grain sea
salt

3 tablespoons fine extra virgin
olive oil

1 jalapeño pepper, seeded and
chopped

1/2 cup chopped red onion

1/2 cup chopped Roma tomato
(about 2 tomatoes)

1/4 cup chopped fresh cilantro

Spicy blue tortilla chips

Plantain chips

• If using fresh peas, bring a pot of water to a boil. Add the peas and cook for 2 to 3 minutes. Remove the peas to an ice bath and submerge until cool; drain. If using frozen peas, thoroughly thaw and continue to next step.

• In a food processor, blend the peas, cumin, lime juice, zest, and salt until all peas are broken down but still a little chunky. You don't want a smooth puree. Stir in the olive oil, jalapeño, and onion.

• Transfer the guacamole to a serving bowl and top with the tomato and cilantro. Serve with chips.

### notes

**Can be made up to twelve hours in advance.** Keep the chips sealed and the guacamole refrigerated until service time.

**Try this recipe** using edamame.

TOTAL TIME: 30 MINUTES / SERVES 8

## corn + tomato *salad*

8 ears corn, shucked

1 teaspoon extra virgin olive oil

1 small red onion, sliced

3 tomatoes, sliced into thin wedges

**DRESSING:**

2 tablespoons fine extra virgin olive oil

1 tablespoon white wine vinegar

1/4 cup chopped fresh cilantro

1/4 cup chopped fresh basil leaves

1/2 teaspoon fine grain sea salt

• Cut the corn kernels from the cob. Set a sauté pan over high heat and add 1 teaspoon olive oil. Add the corn and cook without stirring until charred on one side, about 5 minutes. Let the corn cool to room temperature.

• MAKE THE DRESSING: In a large bowl, whisk together the olive oil, vinegar, cilantro, basil, and salt.

• Toss the corn, onion, and tomatoes in the dressing and serve.

*notes*

**Charring the corn** gives the salad a roasty, more complex flavor. See Quick Reference for information about cutting corn off the cob (page 258) and charring (page 256).

TOTAL TIME: 60 MINUTES / SERVES 10

# collard-wrapped *burritos*

1 teaspoon fine grain sea salt, plus more for blanching water

10 large collard leaves, thickest part of stem trimmed (see Note)

1 3/4 cups water

1 cup quinoa

1 tablespoon extra virgin olive oil

2 teaspoons minced garlic

1/2 teaspoon ground cumin

1/2 teaspoon ground coriander

1 (20-ounce) can black beans, drained

1 carrot, shredded

3 scallions, chopped

2 Roma tomatoes, chopped

1 red bell pepper, chopped

1/4 teaspoon freshly ground black pepper

1 pound sharp cheddar cheese, shredded (about 3 cups)

Olive oil cooking spray

*continued*

• Preheat the oven to 350°F. Spray a 9x13-inch ovenproof serving pan with olive oil. Bring a pot of water to a boil; add a few pinches of salt. Submerge the collards for 2 minutes in boiling water. Drain and set the collard leaves aside.

• In a medium saucepan with a lid, add 1 3/4 cups water and the quinoa. Cook, covered, over medium-low heat for 20 minutes. Set aside and leave covered.

• Meanwhile, heat 1 tablespoon olive oil in a large sauté pan over medium heat. Sauté the garlic, cumin, and coriander for 1 minute. Add the beans, carrot, scallions, tomatoes, bell pepper, salt, and pepper. Let cook for 5 minutes, stirring occasionally. Remove from heat and let cool. Add a splash of water if the mixture gets too dry.

• Lay one collard leaf flat, vein side up. Spoon 2 tablespoons quinoa then 3 tablespoons bean mixture onto the trimmed end of the collard and sprinkle with cheese. Fold each side over the filling and roll like a burrito. Repeat with remaining collard leaves (see photos, opposite page). Arrange the burritos in the serving pan and bake, covered with foil, for 20 minutes or until heated through.

## notes

**When selecting collard greens,** choose the larger leaves that have the fewest holes in them and aren't shriveled at the tops.

**If you can't find large enough collard leaves,** you can secure the wraps with a toothpick to prevent the filling from falling out. Or, use slightly less filling and tell your guests not to limit themselves to just one!

**The quinoa and bean filling** can be cooked one day in advance; store covered in the refrigerator.

**Substitute or omit the cheese** for a vegan dish.

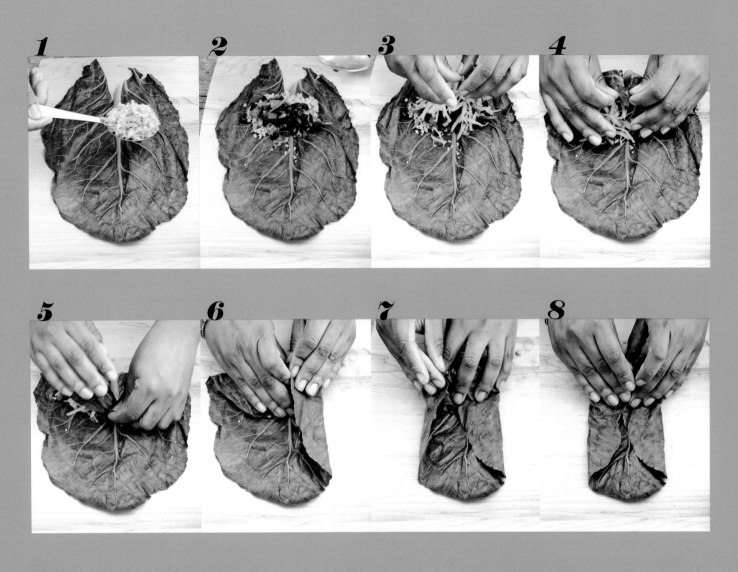

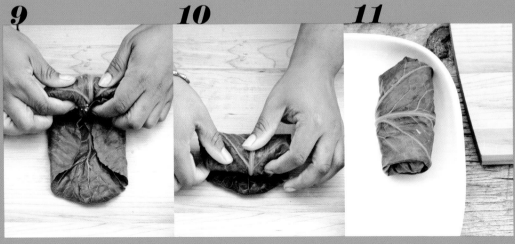

TOTAL TIME: 15 MINUTES / SERVES 10

**S** **V**

## mexican goddess
# chocolate pudding

6 tablespoons cocoa powder

5 ripe Hass avocados

1 cup agave syrup

2 teaspoons pure vanilla extract

1 teaspoon instant espresso powder (optional)

Blackberries or other fresh berries

• In a food processor, puree the cocoa powder, avocados, agave, vanilla, and espresso (if using) until smooth and silky. Add more agave, if necessary, to taste.

• Serve cold, topped with berries.

## notes

**See if your guests** can figure out the secret ingredient with heart-helping good fats.

# menu

|  | SPEEDY | MAKE AHEAD | VEGAN | VEGAN FLEX |
|---|---|---|---|---|
| **edamame dumplings** | | MA | V | |
| **shrimp, bok choy + eggplant stir-fry** | S | | | VF |
| **coconut rice** | | | V | |
| **tatsoi salad with carrot ginger dressing** | S | MA | V | |
| **black sesame brittle** | | MA | | |

***Party Extra: Make togarashi popcorn!*** Shichimi togarashi is a Japanese seven-spice made up of dried peppers, sesame seeds, and nori, among other Asian flavors. Pop popcorn as instructed on page 187, then toss with the togarashi. Your guests can nibble while you finish up the dumplings.

## WINE PAIRING

The subtle floral aromas and melon flavors of good Ginjo or Daiginjo sake work in perfect harmony with the piquant ginger, sweet shrimp, and coconut elements in this breezy meal. Dewazakura, Masumi, and Kaika are producers to look for here. If sake doesn't cut it for you, try a cool German Riesling; keep things fresh and lively with those labeled Kabinett, or salve your sweet tooth with wines labeled Spätlese.

## COOKING ORDER

*1.* brittle
*2.* dumplings
*3.* rice
*4.* salad
*5.* stir-fry

## WARDROBE CHANGE

Change after you've made the sauce for the stir-fry. Boil the dumplings, then add the vegetables and shrimp to the stir-fry before serving. Wear something dark: Between the dipping sauce, the carrot-colored dressing, and the stir-fry, be prepared for spills and splashes.

TOTAL TIME: 1 HOUR, 20 MINUTES / MAKES 24

# edamame dumplings

**DIPPING SAUCE:**

*1/2 cup reduced-sodium soy sauce*

*2 tablespoons sesame oil*

*2 teaspoons red chile pepper flakes*

*2 scallions, chopped*

*2 teaspoons grated fresh ginger*

**DUMPLINGS:**

*1 1/4 cups thinly sliced shiitake mushrooms*

*1 tablespoon vegetable oil, plus more for pan-frying*

*1/8 teaspoon fine grain sea salt*

*3 carrots, shredded*

*1 cup shelled edamame*

*1 teaspoon sesame oil*

*24 wonton wrappers*

• MAKE THE DIPPING SAUCE: Stir together the soy sauce, sesame oil, chile flakes, scallions, and ginger. Set aside.

• MAKE THE DUMPLINGS: In a sauté pan over medium heat, sauté the mushrooms with 1 tablespoon vegetable oil and salt until the mushrooms soften, about 5 minutes. Add the carrots, edamame, and sesame oil. Continue to cook, stirring, for an additional 4 minutes.

• Place 1 teaspoon filling in the center of each wonton wrapper, wet the edges of the wrapper with water, and fold diagonally over the filling, sealing the edges. Wet the opposing corners, fold them in towards each other, and press to seal (see photos, opposite page). The wontons can be frozen at this point, separated by parchment paper, or cooked right away (do not refrigerate the wontons, they may get soggy).

• To cook, bring a pot of water to boil. Add the wontons in batches, reduce the heat, and simmer for 5 minutes. Or, pan-fry them: Add a thin layer of vegetable oil to a sauté pan over medium heat. Cook the dumplings in batches of 8, 3 minutes per side. Serve with the dipping sauce on the side.

## notes

*Frozen edamame* also works for this recipe.

*Wonton wrappers* are usually kept near the tofu or in the international food aisle in the grocery.

*These can get a little chewy if you cook them too early.* Get them ready to go, then store them in a freezer-safe container, separated by parchment paper. Cook them up as your guests begin to trickle in. You can even make them up to a week in advance and freeze them, uncooked.

1

2

3

4

5

6

7

8

TOTAL TIME: 30 MINUTES / SERVES 8

**S** **VF**

# shrimp, bok choy + eggplant *stir-fry*

*1 head bok choy, chopped*

*2 Japanese eggplants, cut into 1-inch cubes (about 4 cups)*

*1 tablespoon grated fresh ginger*

*1 tablespoon minced garlic*

*1 tablespoon vegetable oil*

*3/4 cup light coconut milk*

*1/4 cup reduced-sodium soy sauce*

*2 tablespoons honey*

*1 pound (24 count) shrimp, peeled and deveined*

*2 cups sliced scallions*

*1/2 cup shredded Thai basil leaves, loosely packed*

• Bring a large pot of water to a boil. Blanch the bok choy and eggplants for 1 minute. Drain and set aside.

• In a large sauté pan over medium-high heat, sauté the ginger and garlic in vegetable oil until fragrant, 1 minute. Add the coconut milk and cook for 2 minutes, stirring. Add the soy sauce and honey. Bring to a simmer and then add the shrimp, bok choy and eggplant, and scallions. Simmer until cooked through, about 5 minutes. Stir in the Thai basil and serve with Coconut Rice (page 112).

## notes

*Japanese eggplants* are thinner and usually a paler purple. If you can't find them, use regular eggplants. One would do.

*If you can't find Thai basil,* use a mix of regular basil and mint to achieve a similar taste.

*Make this dish vegan* by substituting tofu for the shrimp.

TOTAL TIME: 45 MINUTES / SERVES 8

# coconut rice

2 cups brown jasmine rice

1 (13 1/2-ounce) can light coconut milk (about 2 cups)

2 cups water

1/2 teaspoon fine grain sea salt

• In a medium saucepan with a lid, stir all ingredients together. Bring to a boil, reduce heat to low, cover, and cook for 40 minutes. Remove from heat and give the rice a light stir with a fork before serving.

## notes

**Jasmine rice** is a fragrant variety of rice from Asia. Use plain brown rice if you can't find it.

**Spice up your rice** if you're in the mood. Drop in a few cardamom pods, a cinnamon stick, and a star anise while simmering. Just don't forget to remove them before serving.

TOTAL TIME: 20 MINUTES / SERVES 8

# *tatsoi salad*
## *with carrot ginger dressing*

**DRESSING:**

1/2 cup chopped carrots

2 tablespoons grated fresh ginger

1 tablespoon sesame oil

1/4 cup plus 1 tablespoon rice vinegar

3 tablespoons extra virgin olive oil

2 tablespoons reduced-sodium soy sauce

1 shallot

2 tablespoons agave syrup


1 English cucumber, thinly sliced

1 pint cherry tomatoes, halved

4 cups tatsoi lettuce, cleaned

• MAKE THE DRESSING: Puree ingredients together in a blender until smooth.

• In a salad bowl, arrange the cucumbers and tomatoes among the lettuce. Drizzle the dressing over the salad and serve.

*notes*

*Tatsoi* has a sweet, mild flavor with a slightly mustardy, pungent aftertaste. If you can't find tatsoi, any green will do— arugula, baby spinach, or watercress might be easier to find.

*The dressing* can be made one day in advance; store covered in the refrigerator.

*We are obsessed with this dressing!* You can also serve it as a dip for vegetables. It's so healthy!

TOTAL TIME: 25 MINUTES / MAKES 2 CUPS, ABOUT 10 SERVINGS

MA

# *black sesame brittle*

*1 cup turbinado or raw sugar*

*2 tablespoons water*

*2 tablespoons unsalted butter*

*2 tablespoons corn syrup*

*1/2 teaspoon flaky sea salt, such as Maldon*

*1 teaspoon black sesame seeds*

• In a saucepan, boil the sugar and water until the sugar darkens, 1 to 2 minutes. Add the butter and corn syrup and return to a boil. Continue to boil, watching carefully, until it darkens to an amber color, about 4 minutes. A candy thermometer should register 350°F.

• Line a cookie sheet with parchment paper. Remove syrup from heat and pour out onto lined cookie sheet. Sprinkle with salt and sesame seeds.

• Let it cool and harden, about 5 minutes, then break into pieces and serve.

## notes

**Make one day in advance** and store in an airtight container.

# menu

| | SPEEDY | MAKE AHEAD | VEGAN | VEGAN FLEX |
|---|---|---|---|---|
| *watercress + pear salad with date vinaigrette* | | MA | V | |
| *braised short ribs with pomegranate onions* | | MA | | |
| *roasted cauliflower salad* | | MA | V | |
| *espresso cinnamon crisps* | | MA | | |
| *the cortez* | | | | VF |

## WINE PAIRING

A hearty Rhône red from Vacqueyras, Gigondas, or Châteauneuf-du-Pape would be a match made in heaven with this savory spread. If these look too pricey, Côtes du Rhône rouges from Domaine Charvin, Domaine de Beaurenard, or Domaine Brusset will also work well for a fraction of the cost.

## COOKING ORDER

*1.* crisps

*2.* short ribs

*3.* cauliflower salad

*4.* pear salad

*5.* cocktail

## WARDROBE CHANGE

After you've composed the cauliflower salad and the components for the pear salad are prepped, change. Then compose the pear salad. Make cocktails to order.

TOTAL TIME: 25 MINUTES / SERVES 8

# *watercress + pear salad*
## *with date vinaigrette*

1/4 cup extra virgin olive oil

1/2 cup apple cider vinegar

1 tablespoon honey

2 tablespoons fresh thyme leaves

1/3 cup chopped, pitted dates

1/2 teaspoon fine grain sea salt

2 hard, ripe pears, such as D'Anjou

Juice from 1 lemon

3 bunches watercress (about 3 pounds), trimmed of tough stems

1/3 cup roasted pepitas

Freshly ground black pepper

• Whisk together the olive oil, vinegar, honey, thyme, dates, and salt. Set aside.

• Slice the pears into matchsticks and toss them in lemon juice to prevent browning and to add a fresh flavor.

• To serve, toss the watercress with the pears and vinaigrette in a large salad bowl. Sprinkle pepitas all over and crack fresh black pepper over the salad.

## notes

*Guess what?* All pepitas are pumpkin seeds but not all pumpkin seeds are pepitas. Pepitas are the shelled, dark green, edible seed of a particular pumpkin.

*The vinaigrette can be made* one day in advance; store covered in the refrigerator.

TOTAL TIME: 3 HOURS / SERVES 10

# *braised short ribs*
## *with pomegranate onions*

5 pounds lean short ribs, with bone (see Note)

1/2 teaspoon fine grain sea salt

1/2 teaspoon freshly ground black pepper

1/4 cup extra virgin olive oil

1 white onion, diced

2 carrots, diced

3 stalks celery, diced

1/4 cup tomato paste

3 cups red wine

2 cups reduced-sodium chicken stock

2 bay leaves

**POMEGRANATE ONIONS:**

3 Vidalia onions, thinly sliced

1/2 cup turbinado or raw sugar

1 tablespoon unsalted butter

24 ounces pomegranate juice (3 cups)

• Preheat the oven to 325°F. Season the short ribs with salt and pepper.

• Place a large, ovenproof, heavy-bottom pan over medium-high heat; add the olive oil. When the oil is hot, sear the short ribs so they're very brown on all sides. Remove ribs to a plate or bowl.

• In the same pan over high heat, sauté the onion, carrots, and celery until they start to brown, about 5 minutes. Add the tomato paste and stir for 1 minute. Deglaze (see Quick Reference, page 258) with red wine. Add the stock and bay leaves. Add the ribs, bone side down. Cover with foil and bake for 2 hours in the oven. Uncover and bake 20 minutes. The ribs should be tender and the sauce should thicken slightly.

• MAKE THE ONIONS: Sweat (sauté without browning) the Vidalia onions, sugar, and butter for 5 minutes in a nonreactive sauté pan over medium heat. Add the pomegranate juice. Cook until the juice is reduced and syrupy, about 10 minutes. Serve the onions over the ribs and on the side.

## *notes*

***Get lean short ribs*** or trim the fat before cooking.

***Use unsweetened pomegranate juice*** so that you control the amount of sweetness that goes into the dish.

***Both the ribs and the onions can be made*** one day in advance and stored separately in the refrigerator. Simply reheat the ribs in a 350°F oven for half an hour and heat the onions over low heat in a saucepan until hot.

TOTAL TIME: 45 MINUTES / SERVES 8 TO 10

# *roasted cauliflower* salad

2 heads cauliflower, chopped into florets

3 tablespoons extra virgin olive oil

1/2 teaspoon fine grain sea salt

3/4 cup crushed walnuts

1/2 cup chopped fresh flat-leaf parsley

1/2 cup chopped fresh cilantro

1/4 cup chopped fresh mint leaves

2 tablespoons chopped fresh oregano

3/4 cup chopped pitted kalamata olives

2 tablespoons juice from the olive jar

2 tablespoons capers packed in brine, crushed

2 teaspoons caper brine

2 tablespoons fresh lemon juice (from about 1 lemon)

2 teaspoons grated lemon zest

1/2 teaspoon freshly ground black pepper

• Preheat the oven to 375°F. Toss the cauliflower with the olive oil and salt. Spread out on a rimmed baking sheet and roast for 20 to 30 minutes or until the edges of the cauliflower are golden brown. Let cool.

• At the same time, spread the walnuts on a rimmed baking sheet and toast in the oven until browned and fragrant, about 10 minutes. Let cool.

• In a large bowl, toss together the cauliflower, walnuts, herbs, and olives.

• In a small bowl, blend the olive juice, capers, caper brine, lemon juice, zest, and pepper. Drizzle the dressing over the cauliflower and toss again. Serve cold or at room temperature.

## *notes*

*If you only have one baking sheet,* toast the nuts, dry, in a pan on the stove. See Quick Reference (page 262).

*This salad can be made* one day in advance; store covered in the refrigerator.

*Jill went through a phase* of being obsessed with cauliflower. Obsessed! This dish is the grand result. You can really add as many or as few herbs as you prefer and the dish will still be phenomenal.

TOTAL TIME: 1 HOUR PLUS CHILLING / MAKES 20 TO 24 COOKIES

MA

# espresso cinnamon *crisps*

*2 cups whole wheat pastry flour*

*3 tablespoons instant espresso powder*

*1/4 teaspoon fine grain sea salt*

*1/4 teaspoon cayenne pepper*

*2 tablespoons ground cinnamon*

*12 tablespoons (1 1/2 sticks) unsalted butter, at room temperature*

*1 cup turbinado or raw sugar*

*1 large egg*

*1 tablespoon pure vanilla extract*

*1/4 cup coarse sugar*

• In a large bowl, mix the flour, 2 tablespoons espresso powder, salt, cayenne, and 1 tablespoon cinnamon. Set aside.

• In another large bowl, cream the butter and turbinado sugar with an electric mixer until fluffy, about 3 minutes. Add the egg and vanilla and beat for another 20 seconds. Stir in the dry ingredients until a dough forms.

• Roll the dough into a 1 1/2-inch diameter log and wrap with plastic wrap. Refrigerate until firm, at least 1 hour or overnight.

## notes

***Although raw sugar*** is somewhat coarse and can be used in a pinch, seeking out coarse sugar will give the cookies a special appearance.

***This dough can be made*** one day in advance and refrigerated.

• Preheat the oven to 350°F. Line a cookie sheet with parchment paper. Mix together the coarse sugar and the remaining 1 tablespoon espresso powder and cinnamon.

• Remove the log from the plastic wrap and roll the log into the sugar mixture to coat the outside. Slice into 1/4-inch-thick rounds.

• Place each cookie about 1 inch apart on the lined cookie sheet. Bake until cookies are firm to the touch, about 10 minutes. Remove cookies to wire racks to cool.

TOTAL TIME: 5 MINUTES / SERVES 2

VF

# *the cortez*

4 ounces bourbon

2 tablespoons fresh lemon juice
(from about 1 lemon)

2 tablespoons honey

Ice

1 cup ginger beer

• Mix the bourbon with lemon and honey. Split the
mixture between 2 rocks glasses. Add ice. Top with
ginger beer.

## *notes*

**Substitute agave syrup** for
honey for a vegan cocktail.

**This drink is best** made to
order. Use drink making as an
excuse to catch-up with a
friend in the kitchen.

daytime

*parties*

*We love to party in the sunlight.* Picnics under falling leaves, beach lunches with friends, and even Mother's Day brunch have proven to be perfect occasions to get together. For the last few years, my family has used Mother's Day as an excuse for a mini New York family reunion. Josie sometimes comes to help out, and we always find ourselves going from bleary-eyed as we start to prep around 9 am to giddy as friends and family start to assemble around noon.

Daytime partying offers an excuse to truly relax with people—there's a communal understanding that the night before may have been a late one and today is all about relaxation and taking things slow. People settle into their spots and enjoy themselves while getting to be with one another. Offer up some great food to complete the laid back vibe! *xo, Jill*

# *menu*

| | SPEEDY | MAKE AHEAD | VEGAN | VEGAN FLEX |
|---|---|---|---|---|
| *minted wheatberry salad with peas* | | MA | | VF |
| *asparagus with poached egg + panko* | | | | |
| *scallops with blood orange citronette* | | | | |
| *coconut rhubarb crumble with raspberry whipped cream* | S | MA | | |

## WINE PAIRING

In addition to white Bordeaux, Austrian Grüner Veltliner has enough personality to pair well with everything here. Even better is the fact that plenty of the best come in crowd-pleasing liter-size bottles.

## COOKING ORDER

*1.* salad

*2.* crumble

*3.* scallops

*4.* asparagus

## WARDROBE CHANGE

Do everything except sear scallops; change, then sear.

TOTAL TIME: 60 MINUTES / SERVES 8

MA VF

# minted *wheatberry salad* with peas

4 cups water

1 cup wheatberries

1/4 cup extra virgin olive oil

1/4 cup fresh lemon juice (from about 2 lemons)

1/2 teaspoon fine grain sea salt

1/2 tablespoon freshly ground black pepper

2 cups fresh peas

2 tablespoons chopped fresh mint leaves

1/2 cup crumbled feta cheese

1/4 teaspoon red chile pepper flakes

1 teaspoon fine extra virgin olive oil

• Place the water and wheatberries in a pot over high heat; bring to a boil. Reduce heat and let simmer until the berries are al dente, about 30 minutes. Drain.

• In a small bowl, mix together 1/4 cup olive oil, the lemon juice, salt, and pepper. Add to the wheatberries while they're warm.

• Bring another pot of water to a boil. Blanch the peas for 3 minutes, then shock in ice water. Drain.

• When the dressed wheatberries are cool, stir in the peas, mint, and feta. Sprinkle with chile flakes and your best olive oil. Serve cold or at room temperature.

## notes

*Wheatberries,* unprocessed, hulled wheat kernels, are available in red and tan varieties. Use either variety in this salad.

*For more information* on blanching, see Quick Reference (page 255).

*This salad can be made* one day in advance; store covered in the refrigerator.

*Omit the cheese* for a vegan dish.

TOTAL TIME: 45 MINUTES / SERVES 12

# *asparagus*
## *with poached egg + panko*

Fine grain sea salt

4 bunches asparagus (about 4 pounds), ends trimmed

2 cups panko breadcrumbs

2 tablespoons grated lemon zest

2 tablespoons extra virgin olive oil

12 large eggs

Truffle salt (optional)

• Bring 4 quarts of water to a boil in a large pot. Add a big pinch of salt. Blanch the asparagus: Drop them in the water, boil for 1 minute, then remove from pot. Quickly rinse the asparagus under cold water until they are room temperature. Slice in half lengthwise.

• In a bowl, mix together the panko and lemon zest. Heat a sauté pan over medium heat. Add the olive oil and panko mixture and toast, stirring, until the mixture takes on a golden color, 3 to 4 minutes. Set aside.

• Fill a shallow saucepan half full with water and bring water to a simmer over medium heat. Poach the eggs by first dropping each one carefully into a cup and then lowering the cup to the water; let the egg gently slip into the water without bursting. Cook for 2 minutes (for runny yolks) in simmering water. If your saucepan is small, poach the eggs in batches.

• Lay the asparagus on a platter. Use a slotted spoon to remove the poached eggs and drain off excess water; place eggs gently on top of the asparagus. Top with the breadcrumbs. Break the yolks to sauce the dish when serving. Finish with a sprinkle of truffle salt, if desired.

## notes

*Try using whole wheat panko* breadcrumbs, if you can find them; look in the Asian food section or near the other breadcrumbs in the grocery aisle.

*If poaching* is just not working for you, you can fry the eggs over easy for the same effect. But first flip to Quick Reference (page 259) for some tips on poaching eggs.

TOTAL TIME: 45 MINUTES / SERVES 6

# *scallops* with *blood orange citronette*

**CITRONETTE:**

*4 cups fresh blood orange juice
(from about 8 oranges)*

*2 tablespoons fine extra virgin
olive oil*

*1/4 teaspoon fine grain sea salt*

*1/4 teaspoon freshly ground
black pepper*

**SCALLOPS:**

*18 large sea scallops*

*1/2 teaspoon fine grain sea salt*

*1/4 teaspoon freshly ground
black pepper*

*1 tablespoon extra-virgin olive
oil*

*2/3 cup microgreens*

• MAKE THE CITRONETTE: Simmer the blood orange juice in a nonreactive saucepan over medium heat until it reduces and thickens into a syrup, about 30 minutes. You should have 3 to 4 tablespoons of syrup when fully reduced. Take the pan off the heat and whisk in the olive oil, salt, and pepper.

• COOK THE SCALLOPS: Season the scallops with salt and pepper. Heat 1 tablespoon olive oil in a sauté pan over high heat. Add the scallops and sear on each side for 2 to 3 minutes.

• Plate the scallops, drizzle with the citronette, and top with microgreens.

## notes

***Blood oranges*** have a short season, about one month in the late winter and are definitely worth seeking out over regular oranges. You can use store-bought blood orange juice, puree, or even soda if you really want to make this dish and can't find fresh blood oranges.

***Don't make the blood orange juice reduction*** too far in advance; it might congeal as it cools and be difficult to get out of the pan.

TOTAL TIME: 45 MINUTES / SERVES 8

- - - - - - - - - - - - - - - - - - - - - - - - - - - - - - - - - - - - - - - - - - - - - - - - - - - - **S** **MA**

# *coconut rhubarb crumble*
## *with raspberry whipped cream*

6 stalks rhubarb, chopped into
1-inch chunks (about 3 cups)

1/2 cup plus 2 tablespoons
turbinado or raw sugar

2 tablespoons fresh lemon juice
(from about 1 lemon)

1 teaspoon grated lemon zest

3 tablespoons unsalted butter,
cold, cut into small pieces

1 cup unsweetened coconut
flakes

1/4 cup whole wheat pastry flour

1/4 cup agave syrup

1 cup cold whipping cream

1 cup raspberries

2 tablespoons confectioners'
sugar

• Preheat the oven to 350°F. Line a 9-inch pie pan with parchment paper.

• Mix the rhubarb with 1/2 cup sugar, the lemon juice, and zest. Mound into the lined pie pan.

• Combine the butter, coconut, flour, agave, and 2 tablespoons sugar in a food processor, pulsing until a soft dough forms. Spread the dough onto the rhubarb evenly. Bake for 30 minutes, until topping is crisp and browned at the edges.

• Pour the cream, berries, and powdered sugar into a cold metal bowl. Whip with a immersion blender until stiff. The berries will break up and turn the cream pink. Serve the crumble warm with whipped cream on the side.

### *notes*

*Try fruit* like berries, apples, or pears when rhubarb is not in season; reduce the sugar accordingly.

*See Quick Reference* for detailed instructions on whipping cream (page 263).

*The crumble can be made* one day in advance; loosely cover with plastic wrap and store in the refrigerator. Reheat in a 300°F oven and whip the cream just before serving.

*Jill learned to make this dish* while working at an organic garden and café outside of Stockholm. She grew and picked the rhubarb herself, and this was one of the rewards she reaped!

*daytime*

# menu

|  | SPEEDY | MAKE AHEAD | VEGAN | VEGAN FLEX |
|---|---|---|---|---|
| *iceberg wedges with honey corn vinaigrette* | S | MA | V | |
| *fried chicken with gravy* | | | | |
| *sharp cheddar + chive waffles* | | | | |
| *hibiscus iced tea* | | MA | V | |

### WINE PAIRING

It's no surprise that these earnest American classics work well with patriotic pours such as Napa Valley Sauvignon Blanc or Pinot Noir from California's central coast, Monterey, or Santa Lucia Highland region. If you're feeling European, juicy Bandol rosé has plenty of stuffing for fried chicken, too.

### COOKING ORDER

*1.* tea
*2.* wedges
*3.* waffles
*4.* chicken

### WARDROBE CHANGE

Frying chicken can be a messy ordeal. Change after you put the chicken in the oven.

TOTAL TIME: 20 MINUTES / SERVES 10

S MA V

# iceberg wedges
## with honey corn vinaigrette

4 ears corn, shucked

Olive oil cooking spray

2 tablespoons honey

1/4 cup golden or white balsamic vinegar

1/4 cup fine extra virgin olive oil

1/2 teaspoon fine grain sea salt

1/2 teaspoon freshly ground black pepper

2 tablespoons fresh basil leaves cut into a chiffonade

1 head iceberg lettuce

• Cut the corn kernels from the cob.

• Place a sauté pan over high heat and spray with olive oil; add the corn. Without stirring, let the corn char slightly, 5 minutes. Remove from heat.

• With a blender, food processor, or immersion blender, mix together the honey, vinegar, olive oil, salt, and pepper. Add half of the corn and process until creamy. Stir in the remaining corn and basil.

• Remove and discard the outer leaves of lettuce, trim the stem, and cut the lettuce head into 10 wedges. Serve the dressing over the wedges.

## notes

**Golden balsamic** has a very similar taste to regular balsamic vinegar. We use it when we don't want dark vinegar coloring the food.

**Don't know how to make a chiffonade?** See Quick Reference (page 256).

**See Quick Reference** for tips on cutting corn off the cob (page 258) and charring (page 256).

**The vinaigrette** can be made one day in advance; store covered in the refrigerator.

TOTAL TIME: 1 HOUR PLUS MARINATING / SERVES 10

- - - - - - - - - - - - - - - - - - - - - - - - - - - - - - - - - - - - - - - - - - - - - - - - - - - - - - - - - - - - - - - - - - - - - - - - - - - - - - - - - - - - - - - - - - - -

# *fried chicken* *with gravy*

**CHICKEN:**

*"The Colonel" spice mix
(page 244)*

*3 cups brown rice flour*

*1 quart buttermilk*

*4 pounds boneless chicken
thighs and breasts (breasts cut
in half)*

*Vegetable oil, for frying*

**GRAVY:**

*6 tablespoons brown rice flour*

*1/4 cup extra virgin olive oil*

*2 cups low-sodium chicken
stock*

• PREPARE THE CHICKEN: In a plastic or paper bag, mix 1 1/2 tablespoons of the spice mix with the rice flour. Set aside. Reserve 2 teaspoons spice mix for the gravy.

• In a large bowl, combine the remainder of the spice mix with the buttermilk. In a sealable plastic bag, marinate the chicken in the buttermilk mixture for 4 hours or overnight in the refrigerator.

• COOK THE CHICKEN: Preheat the oven to 350°F. Line a rimmed baking sheet with foil and set a cooling rack on top. Heat a large pot filled with 1 inch of olive oil to about 350°F.

• Shake the buttermilk off of a piece of chicken and place the chicken in the bag of flour. Shake the bag to coat the chicken.

• Carefully drop each piece of chicken into the oil and fry until the crust is crispy on all sides, 8 to 10 minutes. You can fry several pieces at a time; just be sure not to crowd the pan. Repeat with remaining chicken.

• Remove the chicken from the pot and place on the cooling rack. Place in the oven and bake for 10 minutes, allowing the excess fat to drip onto the cookie sheet. Keep warm in a 300°F oven until ready to serve.

• MAKE THE GRAVY: Stir together the flour and olive oil in a saucepan. Over low heat, cook the mixture, stirring, until it reaches a tan color, about 5 minutes. Carefully pour in the chicken stock and stir until smooth. Add the reserved spice mix and increase the heat to medium. Continue cooking for 10 minutes. Remove from heat. Use an immersion blender to blend the gravy on high speed for 1 minute. Pour the gravy over chicken.

## notes

*If you don't have a thermometer,* you can use breadcrumbs to test the oil. See Quick Reference (page 262) for more information.

*The chicken can marinate overnight.* This is a great make-ahead opportunity.

*Baking the chicken after a quick fry* removes a lot of excess oil and keeps the chicken juicy. If you want to fry the chicken completely, fry in the oil for 20 minutes and skip the oven step.

*This recipe is gluten free* (provided your chicken stock is also); allergic friends will be thrilled! And, as a bonus, the rice flour actually makes the chicken crispier.

TOTAL TIME: 50 MINUTES / SERVES 12 (MAKES ABOUT 5 WAFFLES)

# sharp cheddar + chive *waffles*

2 large eggs, separated

1 1/2 cups shredded
extra-sharp cheddar cheese

3 tablespoons chopped chives

1 1/2 teaspoons maple syrup

1 3/4 cups whole wheat pastry
flour or gluten-free all-purpose
flour (see Note)

1 tablespoon baking powder

1/4 teaspoon fine grain sea salt

1 3/4 cups buttermilk

1/4 cup extra virgin olive oil

Olive oil cooking spray

• In a clean, large bowl, whip the egg whites to firm peaks with an electric mixer.

• Combine the remaining ingredients (except the cooking spray) in a separate large bowl. Lightly but thoroughly fold the egg whites into the other batter ingredients.

• Make waffles per machine instructions, spraying with olive oil if necessary. The waffles should be golden brown and crisp. Serve with fried chicken and gravy.

## notes

*If you're interested in a gluten-free menu,* use gluten-free flour for the waffles.

*No waffle iron?* Simply mix all ingredients together without whipping the egg whites. Make pancakes instead on a warm griddle or frying pan.

*Recrisp and warm* in a 300°F oven on a cookie sheet for 5 minutes, if necessary.

TOTAL TIME: 20 MINUTES PLUS STEEPING + CHILLING / MAKES 12 CUPS

MA V

# hibiscus iced tea

1 1/2 teaspoons grated fresh ginger

1/4 teaspoon ground allspice

12 cups water

2 ounces dried hibiscus flowers (see Note)

1/2 cup turbinado or raw sugar

• In a medium saucepan over medium heat, simmer the ginger, allspice, and water for 15 minutes. Remove from heat. Add the hibiscus, stir, and cover.

• Let the flowers steep for 2 hours. Add the sugar to taste; stir. Strain, chill, and serve over ice.

## notes

**Hibiscus** for this recipe should be dried and unsweetened—meant for tea, not for snacking. If you have trouble finding it, see our Sources (page 264).

**This tea can keep** in the fridge for up to three days before it starts to lose its tang, but it's best made the day before.

**Turn this drink into a cocktail** by adding rum, vodka, or an effervescent wine.

# menu

|  | SPEEDY | MAKE AHEAD | VEGAN | VEGAN FLEX |
|---|---|---|---|---|
| *seafood cobb* | | | | |
| *green goddess purple potatoes* | |  | |  |
| *spiced stone fruit salad* | |  |  | |

## WINE PAIRING

Fresh white wine such as Spanish Albariño from the Rias Baixas or citrusy Verdelho from Rueda pair perfectly with fresh seafood and tangy greens, and most have enough weight to work well with heartier ingredients, too.

## COOKING ORDER

*1.* fruit salad

*2.* seafood cobb

*3.* potatoes

## WARDROBE CHANGE

Keep the potatoes warm in the oven, change, and then plate them when guests arrive. Add the avocado to your salad at this time.

TOTAL TIME: 60 MINUTES / SERVES 10

# seafood cobb

2 cups dry white wine

1 lemon, sliced

1/2 teaspoon fine grain sea salt

1/2 teaspoon whole black peppercorns

1/2 pound shrimp (30 count or smaller), peeled and deveined

6 strips bacon (optional)

2 heads Bibb lettuce, washed, dried, and torn

1/4 cup fresh tarragon leaves

1/4 cup chopped chives

1/2 pound fine packaged tuna in olive oil, drained

2 tomatoes, diced

1/2 pound fresh crab meat, picked through for shells

4 hard-boiled eggs (see Quick Reference, page 258), chopped

2 tablespoons Dijon mustard

1/2 cup tarragon vinegar

1/2 cup extra virgin olive oil

Freshly ground black pepper

2 ripe Hass avocados

2 tablespoons fresh lemon juice (from about 1 lemon)

• Fill a large saucepan 2/3 full with water. Add the white wine, lemon slices, salt, and peppercorns. Simmer for 10 minutes over medium-high heat. Add the shrimp and turn off the heat. Let the shrimp sit in the poaching liquid for 15 minutes. Drain and let shrimp cool in the refrigerator.

• In a sauté pan over medium-low heat, cook the bacon until crispy, flipping occasionally, about 15 minutes. Drain on a paper towel and roughly chop into small pieces. Set aside.

• Toss the lettuce with the tarragon leaves and chives and spread out on a large platter. Arrange the tuna, tomatoes, crab, shrimp, eggs, and bacon on top of the lettuce in rows, leaving a space open for the avocado.

• In a small bowl, mix the Dijon, tarragon vinegar, and olive oil. Drizzle on top of the salad or serve on the side.

• Chop the avocados and gently mix with 2 tablespoons lemon juice. Just before the guests arrive add the avocados to the salad.

## notes

**The lemon juice** helps keep the avocado from turning brown, but even so, be sure not to chop it too early.

**Fresh tuna,** seared on all sides would also work well with this dish. Season to taste with salt and pepper.

TOTAL TIME: 60 MINUTES / SERVES 10

MA VF

## green goddess
# purple potatoes

3 pounds purple potatoes (see Note)

1 tablespoon extra virgin olive oil

1/2 teaspoon fine grain sea salt

**GREEN GODDESS DRESSING:**

1 cup silken tofu

1 cup chopped chives

1 cup fresh basil leaves

1/2 cup fresh tarragon leaves

2 tablespoons grated lemon zest

1/4 cup fresh lemon juice (from about 1 lemon)

1 tablespoon prepared horseradish

1/2 teaspoon fine grain sea salt

1/2 teaspoon freshly ground black pepper

1/2 cup sour cream

1/2 teaspoon flaky sea salt, such as Maldon

• Preheat the oven to 400°F. Chop the potatoes into 1-inch cubes. Toss them with the olive oil and salt and spread onto a rimmed baking sheet. Roast until fork tender, 30 to 45 minutes, stirring halfway through the cooking time.

• MAKE THE DRESSING: In a blender, puree all the dressing ingredients except sour cream together until fairly smooth. Fold in the sour cream.

• Remove the potatoes from the oven and sprinkle with flaky sea salt.

• Serve the warm potatoes with the dressing either on the side or drizzled over top.

### notes

*If you can't get purple potatoes,* you can certainly substitute red bliss, Yukon golds, fingerlings, etc.

*The dressing can be made* up to one day in advance; store covered in the refrigerator.

*Keep the potatoes warm* in a 250°F oven for up to thirty minutes.

*The salad can be made vegan* with the substitution of vegan sour cream.

TOTAL TIME: 25 MINUTES / SERVES 10

# spiced stone fruit salad

12 mixed stone fruits (plums, apricots, peaches, white peaches, pluots, etc.)

3 green cardamom pods

1/4 cup fresh lime juice (from about 4 limes)

1 teaspoon grated fresh ginger

1/4 cup agave syrup

1 star anise

1 cup water

1/4 cup small fresh basil leaves, for garnish

• Pit and slice all the stone fruit. Set aside in a bowl.

• Smash the cardamom pods with a pan or side of a knife just a little to open them up. Add the cardamom, lime juice, ginger, agave, star anise, and water to a saucepan. Simmer for 15 minutes over low heat. Let cool.

• Strain the liquid over the fruit; stir lightly. Refrigerate until ready to serve. Garnish with basil leaves.

## notes

*If you get the freestone variety of stone fruit,* they'll be easier to pit. Otherwise, just cut around the pit to keep your salad pretty.

*The smaller basil leaves* are generally at the top of the stem in the center.

*Agave syrup's* light flavor and juicy sweetness is perfect for this dish.

*The dressing for the fruit can be prepared* one day in advance, but the salad shouldn't sit around for more than six hours. Store both covered in the refrigerator.

| | SPEEDY | MAKE AHEAD | VEGAN | VEGAN FLEX |
|---|---|---|---|---|
| *the granola mash-up* | | MA | V | |
| *baked eggs over spinach* | S | | | |
| *challah french toast with honeyed ricotta + blueberry vanilla jam* | | MA | | |
| *onion tart with gruyère crust* | | MA | | |

---

### WINE PAIRING

Sparkling wines work best at brunch and you don't need to break the bank to find something worth toasting over French toast. Look for Spanish Cava, Italian Prosecco, or Gruet's bargain-priced sparkler from New Mexico.

### COOKING ORDER

*1.* granola
*2.* tart
*3.* French toast
*4.* eggs

### WARDROBE CHANGE

Put the eggs in the oven then change. You won't have a ton of time, so attend to "bed head" before starting this menu.

TOTAL TIME: 40 MINUTES / MAKES ABOUT 5 CUPS

# the *granola* mash-up

3 cups thick-cut rolled oats

1/4 cup wheat germ

2 tablespoons white sesame seeds

1 tablespoon black sesame seeds

1 cup slivered almonds

3/4 cup chopped walnuts

1/4 teaspoon ground cinnamon

1/4 teaspoon fine grain sea salt

1/3 cup extra virgin olive oil

6 tablespoons maple syrup

1/2 cup golden raisins

1/4 cup dried cherries

• Preheat the oven to 350°F. In a large bowl, stir together the oats, wheat germ, both sesame seeds, almonds, walnuts, cinnamon, and salt. Add the olive oil and 3 tablespoons maple syrup, stirring until thoroughly combined.

• Spread the mix evenly on a rimmed baking sheet and bake for 20 minutes, stirring after the first 10 minutes. After 20 minutes, remove from the oven and stir in the remaining 3 tablespoons maple syrup. Return to the oven for 10 more minutes. Granola should be golden brown and fairly crisp, cooking for about 30 minutes total.

• Let the granola cool on the cookie sheet. Stir in the raisins and cherries. Allow to cool completely, then store in an airtight jar. Serve with fruit and yogurt.

## notes

**The second addition of maple syrup** makes the granola glossier and creates more of those yummy clumps.

**Jill likes to add more cinnamon,** many types of almonds (slivered, sliced, and whole), and she toasts hers until it's very dark.

**Josie doesn't add cinnamon,** likes to add unsweetened coconut, and toasts hers lighter. This recipe is our combined love, but you can always make variations to personalize it!

**The granola keeps fresh for almost a month** if you store it in an airtight container, so make plenty.

TOTAL TIME: 30 MINUTES / SERVES 10

S

# baked eggs *over spinach*

*Olive oil cooking spray*

*2 pounds baby spinach (about 8 cups)*

*1 cup walnut halves*

*1/2 cup freshly grated Parmesan cheese*

*1/2 teaspoon ground nutmeg*

*2 cloves garlic*

*1/4 teaspoon freshly ground black pepper*

*6 tablespoons whole milk*

*10 large eggs*

• Preheat the oven to 350°F. Spray a 9x13-inch baking dish with olive oil.

• Bring a pot of water to a boil. Blanch the spinach for 30 seconds. Drain, rinse with cold water, then squeeze out most of the water.

• In a food processor, pulse half of the spinach with the walnuts, Parmesan, nutmeg, garlic, and pepper for 20 seconds. It should still be a little chunky but evenly chopped. Quickly stir in the rest of spinach and the milk. Cover the bottom of the baking dish with this mixture.

• Crack the eggs over the spinach, keeping the eggs whole and close to one another.

• Bake uncovered for 15 minutes for soft set eggs (see Note). Eggs might look glossy and a little undercooked, but they aren't.

## notes

***Frozen spinach will also work*** just fine for this dish, and it'll save you time. No need to blanch it, just thaw and use!

***This recipe will work with skim milk*** if you want a lower calorie dish. It also works with cream if you want the dish to be very luxurious!

***Blanching*** is an important step to keep your greens their greenest while cooking. In this recipe, it also removes excess water from the spinach. See Quick Reference (page 255) for further description on blanching.

***If you like your eggs firmer*** and not runny, let them bake for 20 to 25 minutes.

TOTAL TIME: 60 MINUTES PLUS COOLING / SERVES 10

------------------------------------------------

# *challah french toast*
## *with honeyed ricotta + blueberry vanilla jam*

**JAM:**

5 cups blueberries

1 vanilla bean, split and seeded
(see Note)

2 tablespoons fresh lemon juice
(from about 1 lemon)

1/2 cup turbinado or raw sugar

**RICOTTA:**

16 ounces ricotta cheese

1 tablespoon honey

**FRENCH TOAST:**

3 large eggs

4 cups milk

1 cup turbinado or raw sugar

1/2 teaspoon pure vanilla
extract

1/2 teaspoon ground cinnamon

10 (1-inch) slices challah bread

3 tablespoons unsalted butter or
olive oil cooking spray

• MAKE THE JAM: In a medium saucepan over medium-low heat, simmer the blueberries, vanilla pod and seeds, lemon juice, and sugar, uncovered, until thick, stirring occasionally, 30 to 45 minutes. Remove the vanilla pod and let the jam cool in the pan for at least an hour.

• PREPARE THE RICOTTA: Place the ricotta in a strainer over a bowl for 20 to 30 minutes to remove the excess water. Discard the water. Place the ricotta in the bowl and add the honey; stir to combine. Cover and refrigerate until ready to serve.

• MAKE THE FRENCH TOAST: In a large bowl, combine the eggs, milk, sugar, vanilla, and cinnamon.

• Heat a skillet or griddle over medium-low heat. Add some of the butter or cooking spray and swirl to cover the pan. Dip a slice of bread into the batter. Let the bread sit until it's heavy with the batter but not falling apart (about 30 seconds). Once the butter is hot, brown the bread on both sides, about 5 minutes each side. Repeat until all the bread is used. Add butter or spray to the pan between batches to keep the toast from sticking. Serve French toast with ricotta and jam.

## notes

*You can use vanilla extract in the jam,* but vanilla bean makes this dish ambrosial. See our Sources (page 264) for vanilla bean purveyors. The equivalent of one vanilla bean is about 2 teaspoons vanilla extract.

*Fresh or frozen berries* work fine here.

*Lemon juice brightens the flavor of the jam* and adds additional natural pectin, important for thickening the jam.

*If your griddle gets too hot,* it may be necessary to turn down the heat or remove the pan from the heat entirely. Cast iron pans retain heat very well, so pay attention.

*If you need to keep your toasts warm,* keep them loosely covered with foil in a 200°F oven.

*The jam can be made* up to two weeks in advance. The ricotta, one day in advance; store both in airtight containers in the refrigerator.

TOTAL TIME: 2 HOURS / SERVES 10 TO 12

--------------------------------------------------------------------------------

# *onion tart* *with gruyère crust*

**FILLING:**

2 tablespoons unsalted butter

1 tablespoon extra virgin olive oil

6 Vidalia onions, thinly sliced

1 teaspoon fine grain sea salt

3 large eggs

1 cup milk

1/8 teaspoon ground nutmeg

2 tablespoons chopped fresh flat-leaf parsley

**CRUST:**

1 cup shredded Gruyère cheese

2 cups whole wheat pastry flour, plus more for dusting

1/2 teaspoon fine grain sea salt

8 tablespoons (1 stick) cold unsalted butter, cut into small pieces

1/4 cup cold water

MA

• MAKE THE FILLING: Place a large sauté pan over medium-low heat; melt the butter with the olive oil. Add the onions and 1/4 teaspoon salt and sauté until onions are very soft and medium brown, 30 to 45 minutes. Let the onions cool to room temperature.

• In a bowl, mix together the eggs, milk, nutmeg, parsley, and remaining 3/4 teaspoon salt. Add half of this mixture to the cooled onions. Set aside.

• MAKE THE CRUST: Preheat the oven to 400°F. While the onions cook, place the cheese, flour, and salt in a food processor. Pulse for 20 seconds to combine. Cut the butter into the flour by pulsing for 15 seconds. Add the water and continue to pulse until the dough comes together. Chill the dough for 10 minutes. It should have a little resistance when poked with your finger but still be easy to roll out.

• Roll out the dough on a floured surface until it's about 1/8-inch thick and lay it in a 9- or 10-inch pie pan. Pinch the edges of the dough for a decorative pattern and trim the excess. Add the onion filling and top off with the remainder of the egg mixture so that it fills to edge of the crust. Cut 2-inch strips of foil and cover the crimped edges loosely so the crust doesn't burn. Discard any extra dough or egg mixture.

• Bake until the center of the filling is firm and doesn't jiggle when you move the pan, about 45 minutes. Let it cool for 15 minutes and serve.

## notes

*Vidalia onions* have a milder, sweeter flavor than the average yellow onion.

*Feel free to experiment with other hard cheeses,* such as Asiago, Parmesan, or a 2-year aged cheddar, for the crust.

*If you don't have a food processor,* use a pastry cutter to cut the butter into the dry ingredients.

*To save time,* caramelize the onions one day in advance and store them in the refrigerator.

*The dough for the crust can also be made one day in advance* and refrigerated (or even frozen). Wrap the dough in plastic wrap. Before rolling, let it sit at room temperature for 30 minutes.

*party*

*of two*

*Sometimes your reason for celebration doesn't warrant a crowd.* With these scaled-down recipes, you can create a special meal for a more intimate party. The quantities can easily be doubled for an evening with your closest friends or a visit from family. Think of these menus when you want to create a memorable moment with the beau, a personal tribute to Mom or Dad, or a celebratory feast for two long-time friends. *xo, Josie*

# menu

|  | SPEEDY | MAKE AHEAD | VEGAN | VEGAN FLEX |
|---|---|---|---|---|
| *fennel salad with grapefruit vinaigrette* | S | | V | |
| *filet mignon with wedding sauce* | | MA | | |
| *truffle-laced potatoes with artichoke hearts + leeks* | | | V | |
| *crispy chocolate banana bread pudding* | | MA | | |

## WINE PAIRING

A citrus-scented Sauvignon Blanc from the Russian River Valley is a great match for the salad, while a decadent Paso Robles red syncs magically with the filet—look for spicy Zinfandel or Syrah for best results.

## COOKING ORDER

1. bread pudding
2. salad
3. potatoes
4. filet

## WARDROBE CHANGE

Prepare everything but the steaks. Sear them but don't put them in the oven until you're almost ready to serve. You can change right after searing.

TOTAL TIME: 25 MINUTES / SERVES 2

S V

# *fennel salad*
## *with grapefruit vinaigrette*

1 fennel bulb

2 radishes

1/4 red onion

1 grapefruit, suprêmed (see
Quick Reference, page 260)

1 tablespoon sherry vinegar

1/4 teaspoon fine grain sea salt

2 tablespoons fine extra virgin
olive oil

Toasted pepitas or sunflower
seeds, for garnish

• Slice the fennel, radishes, and red onion on a
mandoline. They should be almost paper-thin. Set aside.

• Make the grapefruit vinaigrette
by mixing the grapefruit sections
and juice, vinegar, salt, and olive
oil together. Gently toss the
dressing and salad together and
serve with a sprinkle of pepitas or
sunflower seeds on top.

*notes*

**When sectioning the
grapefruit**, work over a bowl
to save all of the juice from the
fruit.

**This recipe is a great one for
testing out your mandoline.**
It makes for a more artful
presentation and a tastier end
result. If you don't have a
mandoline, it's a good time to
start practicing your knife skills!

TOTAL TIME: 25 MINUTES / SERVES 2

# *filet mignon* *with wedding sauce*

1 shallot, sliced

1 cup port wine

1/3 cup balsamic vinegar

1/2 teaspoon freshly ground black pepper

1 tablespoon unsalted butter

1 tablespoon extra virgin olive oil

2 (1-inch-thick) filet mignon steaks (about 1/2 pound each)

Fine grain sea salt (optional)

• Preheat the oven to 400°F. In a small nonreactive saucepan over low heat, combine the shallots, port, vinegar, and pepper; cook until reduced to about 1/4 cup, 15 to 20 minutes. Stir in the butter.

• While the sauce is reducing, heat an ovenproof sauté pan over high heat; add the olive oil. Sear both sides of the steaks, about 2 minutes each side. Drain off the oil and place the pan with the steaks in the oven for about 5 minutes for medium steaks.

• To serve, plate the steaks and pour the sauce over top. Crack fresh black pepper and sprinkle salt over the steak, if desired.

## notes

**The sauce can be made one day in advance**—minus the butter. Store covered in the refrigerator. When it's time to serve, rewarm the sauce and then stir in the butter.

**The sauce is named "Wedding Sauce"** because we once made it for a wedding. Guests, as well as the bride and groom, raved! Keep the official name of the dish to yourself if you think it hints too much at commitment.

TOTAL TIME: 45 MINUTES / SERVES 2

# truffle-laced *potatoes*
## with artichoke hearts + leeks

1 russet potato, peeled and cut into 1/4-inch slices

1 tablespoon extra virgin olive oil

1 teaspoon truffle salt

1 leek, washed and sliced into 1/4-inch rings (see Quick Reference, page 260)

1/3 cup water

10 ounces frozen artichoke hearts, thawed

• Preheat the oven to 400°F. Toss the potato with 1 1/2 teaspoons olive oil and 1/2 teaspoon truffle salt. Spread onto a rimmed baking sheet and roast in the oven until fork tender and browned, about 35 minutes, flipping the potato once.

• In a large saucepan, heat the remaining 1 1/2 teaspoons olive oil over medium-low heat. Add the leeks and cook for 3 minutes, stirring occasionally. Add the water and artichokes, reduce the heat slightly, cover the pan, and cook for 10 minutes.

• Stir in the roasted potato and the remaining 1/2 teaspoon truffle salt to taste. Let sit for 5 minutes and then serve.

## notes

*If you can't find frozen artichoke hearts*, use canned, drained artichokes. And, of course, you can always use freshly cooked ones!

*To make this into a full meal* in itself, toast couscous, cook it, and mix it with this hearty veggie blend.

TOTAL TIME: 1 HOUR, 10 MINUTES / SERVES 2

MA

## *crispy chocolate banana*
# *bread pudding*

1 brioche roll (about 4 inches wide)

1 ripe banana

1 large egg

1/2 cup milk

1/4 cup turbinado or raw sugar

1 teaspoon pure vanilla extract

1/8 teaspoon ground nutmeg

1/3 cup semisweet chocolate chips

• Preheat the oven to 350°F. Tear the brioche roll into small pieces. Slice the banana into 1/4-inch-thick rounds.

• Mix together the egg, milk, sugar, vanilla, and nutmeg in a medium bowl. Add the bread pieces. Stir in the banana and chocolate chips. Let the mixture soak for 20 minutes.

• Pour into 2 ovenproof bowls or ramekins. Bake for 35 minutes. Let cool for 5 minutes before serving.

### *notes*

*If you can't find brioche rolls,* you can use challah or egg bread and then freeze the remainder of the loaf for another time.

*The bread pudding can be made one day in advance* and warmed in a 350°F oven. Cover with foil or plastic wrap before storing in the refrigerator.

# *menu*

|  | SPEEDY | MAKE AHEAD | VEGAN | VEGAN FLEX |
|---|---|---|---|---|
| *beets with citrus + ginger goat cheese* | | MA | | VF |
| *seafood stew* | | MA | | |
| *apricot shortcakes with five-spice whipped cream* | | MA | | |

## WINE PAIRING

A fragrant white from the Languedoc Rhône Valley should do the trick here. If you're feeling spendy, look for Châteauneuf-du-Pape blanc, or grab a Picpoul de Pinet, one of the world's greatest white wine values and great with seafood stew.

## COOKING ORDER

*1.* shortcakes

*2.* beets

*3.* stew

## WARDROBE CHANGE

Change just after adding stock and water to the stew. You've got about twenty minutes!

TOTAL TIME: 20 MINUTES / SERVES 2

# *beets* **with citrus + ginger goat cheese**

2 ounces fresh goat cheese

1/4 teaspoon grated fresh ginger

1/2 teaspoon grated orange zest

2 medium golden, red, or chiogga beets, peeled (see Note)

1 1/2 tablespoons fine extra virgin olive oil

1 1/2 tablespoons Champagne vinegar

1/4 teaspoon fine grain sea salt

1 orange, suprêmed (see Quick Reference, page 260)

Chopped chives, for garnish

• In a bowl, stir together the goat cheese, ginger, and orange zest with a fork. Set aside, covered, in the refrigerator.

• Slice the beets paper-thin with a mandoline. In a large bowl, stir together the olive oil, vinegar, and salt; add the orange sections and beets and toss.

• To serve, place the beet salad on a plate. Dot with goat cheese and sprinkle with chives.

### *notes*

**Chiogga beets** are the candy-striped beets. Wear kitchen gloves if using red beets to protect your hands from staining.

**You can store sliced beets** in cold water to keep them fresh and crisp until you're ready to serve them.

**The goat cheese mix** can be made one day in advance; store covered in the refrigerator. Make extra to use the next day in afternoon tea sandwiches with sliced cucumbers, pear, and mint.

**To make this a vegan dish,** omit the cheese.

TOTAL TIME: 60 MINUTES / SERVES 2

# seafood stew

1 tablespoon extra virgin olive oil

1 green bell pepper, diced

1 small yellow onion, diced

1/2 teaspoon fine grain sea salt

1/2 cup diced fennel bulb

1 loosely packed teaspoon saffron

1/4 teaspoon red chile pepper flakes

2 cups fish stock

1 cup water

3/4 pound mixed fish or seafood, such as salmon, cod, scallops, shrimp, clams, or mussels

Crusty whole wheat bread

• Heat the olive oil in a sauté pan over medium heat. Sauté the green pepper and onion with salt until the onion is opaque, about 5 minutes. Add the fennel and sauté for another 5 minutes.

• Add the saffron and chile flakes; cook for 2 minutes. Add the stock and water and simmer the broth for 20 minutes on low heat.

• Cut the fish into smaller bite-size pieces, if necessary. Add the seafood all at once and simmer on very low heat for 5 minutes. If using clams or mussels, cook just until the shells open. Discard any that don't open. Serve warm with crusty bread.

## notes

**Prep the broth and vegetables** one day in advance, but add the fish shortly before serving.

**Check out the roasted garlic recipe** on page 75. The garlic will go great on the bread before a dunk in the stew.

TOTAL TIME: 2 HOURS INCLUDING MACERATING / MAKES 4

SEE *photo* PAGE 168

# *apricot shortcakes*
## *with five-spice whipped cream*

4 ripe apricots, pitted and sliced

2 teaspoons turbinado or raw sugar

1/2 teaspoon grated fresh ginger

2 teaspoons fresh lemon juice (from about 1/2 lemon)

**SHORTCAKES:**

1/2 cup whole wheat pastry flour

1/2 teaspoon baking powder

1/4 teaspoon fine grain sea salt

1/4 cup turbinado or raw sugar

2 tablespoons unsalted butter, at room temperature

1 large egg

1/2 teaspoon pure vanilla extract

3 tablespoons milk

**WHIPPED CREAM:**

1/2 cup cold whipping cream

1/4 teaspoon Chinese five-spice powder

*continued*

• In a small bowl, mix together the apricots, sugar, ginger, and lemon juice. Refrigerate for at least 30 minutes or up to 2 hours.

• Preheat the oven to 350°F. Butter 4 cups in a muffin pan. Put a mixing bowl in the freezer to chill.

• MAKE THE SHORTCAKES: Mix together the flour, baking powder, and salt in a small bowl. In a separate medium bowl, whip the sugar and butter with an electric mixer until light and fluffy, about 5 minutes. Add the egg and vanilla and mix until just combined. Add half the flour, all of the milk, then the remaining flour, beating lightly after each addition.

• Pour the batter evenly into muffin cups, about 3/4 full; it should make 4 shortcakes. Bake for 20 minutes or until a toothpick inserted into the middle of a shortcake comes out clean.

• MAKE THE WHIPPED CREAM: Clean the mixer and whip the cream with the five-spice powder in the chilled bowl until peaks form, 3 to 4 minutes.

• To serve, slice shortcakes in half, horizontally. Place the apricots on the bottom halves, and then add a generous dollop of cream. Top with the other half of the cake.

*notes*

*Chinese five-spice powder* is found either in the spice aisle or in the Asian food section of the grocery.

*See Quick Reference* for detailed instructions on whipping cream (page 263).

*You can make the cakes* one day in advance; store in an airtight container.

*This recipe actually makes four servings.* You'll be glad it does. The other two servings can be eaten in the morning. (Wink, wink.)

# *menu*

|  | SPEEDY | MAKE AHEAD | VEGAN | VEGAN FLEX |
|---|---|---|---|---|
| **spinach + cremini split pea soup** | |  |  | |
| **oyster mushroom + sage orzo** |  | | |  |
| **hazelnut budino** | | | | |

## WINE PAIRING

A berry-scented Barbera from Italy's Piedmont region is just the wine for mushrooms. Look for Barbera d'Alba, a wine crafted with grapes harvested from vineyards around the town of Alba, famous for its Fiera del Tartufo Bianco—the Festival of White Truffles.

## COOKING ORDER

*1.* soup

*2.* orzo

*3.* budino

## WARDROBE CHANGE

Prep the budinos, change, then put them in the oven when your guest arrives. The soup will stay warm on the stove while you two enjoy a first glass of wine.

TOTAL TIME: 1 HOUR, 10 MINUTES / SERVES 2 WITH POSSIBLE LEFTOVERS

MA V

*spinach + cremini*
# split pea soup

1 tablespoon extra virgin olive oil

1/2 cup chopped onion

1 carrot, chopped

1 stalk celery, chopped

2 cups vegetable stock

1 cup water

1 bay leaf

1 1/2 teaspoons fresh thyme leaves

1 teaspoon chopped fresh savory

1/2 cup split peas

1 1/2 cups sliced cremini mushrooms (see Note)

1/4 teaspoon fine grain sea salt

1/4 teaspoon freshly ground pepper

2 cups baby spinach

1/2 teaspoon sherry vinegar (optional)

• In a large saucepan over medium heat, heat the olive oil. Sauté the onion, carrot, and celery for 5 minutes. Add the stock, water, bay leaf, thyme, savory, split peas, and mushrooms. Bring to a boil and then simmer, covered, for 1 hour or until the peas are tender and mash easily when stirred. Check the liquid during cooking; add more stock and/or water, if necessary. Add salt and pepper.

• Once the peas are soft, add the spinach, stir for 1 minute, and remove from heat. Stir in the sherry vinegar, if using, and serve.

## notes

*Cremini mushrooms* are also known as baby portabellas or baby bellas.

*This soup can be made one day in advance;* store covered in the refrigerator. You'll need to add water when reheating; it thickens when cooled.

TOTAL TIME: 45 MINUTES / SERVES 2

# *oyster mushroom + sage* ORZO

*Fine grain sea salt*

*2/3 cup orzo*

*1 shallot, chopped*

*1 tablespoon extra virgin olive oil, plus more for drizzling*

*1/2 pound oyster mushrooms, chopped*

*2 fresh sage leaves, chopped*

*2 tablespoons chopped sun-dried tomatoes*

*1 teaspoon grated lemon zest*

*3 anchovies, chopped*

*1/4 cup freshly grated Pecorino Romano cheese*

*1/3 cup crushed walnuts, toasted*

• Fill a medium pot 2/3 full with water, add salt, and bring to a boil. Add the orzo and cook until al dente, about 7 minutes. Drain, reserving 1/2 cup of the pasta water.

• Meanwhile, in a large sauté pan over medium heat, sauté the shallot in 1 tablespoon olive oil for 2 minutes. Turn down the heat and add the mushrooms and sage and cook until the mushrooms are wilted and start to brown on the edges, about 10 minutes. Add the pasta and 1/2 cup pasta water to the sauté pan. Toss in the sun-dried tomatoes, lemon zest, anchovies, cheese, and walnuts and remove from heat.

• Drizzle with olive oil to serve.

## *notes*

*Omit the pecorino and anchovies* for a vegan dish. Add a little salt to account for the missing cheese and fish.

*Jill makes a version of this every week.* No one ever notices the anchovies, but they do notice the delicious, hard-to-pinpoint savoriness!

TOTAL TIME: 35 MINUTES / SERVES 2

# *hazelnut budino*

4 teaspoons unsalted butter, at room temperature, plus more for ramekins

1/4 cup peeled hazelnuts, toasted (see Quick Reference, pages 259, 262)

1/4 cup milk chocolate chips

1/4 cup turbinado or raw sugar

1 large egg, separated

1/4 teaspoon fine grain sea salt

1/2 teaspoon pure vanilla extract

• Preheat the oven to 350°F. Butter 2 ovenproof ramekins. Pulse the hazelnuts in a food processor until they are finely ground. The smoother this is, the smoother your budino will be.

• Place the chocolate and butter in a microwave-safe bowl and microwave on the defrost setting or 50% power for 30 seconds or until melted. Stir to combine.

• Add the crushed hazelnuts, 2 tablespoons sugar, the egg yolk, salt, and vanilla extract to the chocolate-butter mixture and mix until combined.

• In a clean bowl, beat the egg white with an electric mixer until soft peaks form. Slowly add the remaining 2 tablespoons sugar and continue beating until the sugar has dissolved and the egg white stands stiff.

• Gently fold the egg white into the chocolate mixture. Spoon the batter into ramekins. Bake until the tops puff up and become stiff, about 20 minutes.

## *notes*

*When whisking egg whites,* be sure your bowl and whisk are free of fat (like butter or oil). They prevent the whites from airing to their full potential.

*These are great served* with vanilla ice cream or a cappuccino.

*Don't make these ahead of time;* the budino will fall.

# menu

| | SPEEDY | MAKE AHEAD | VEGAN | VEGAN FLEX |
|---|---|---|---|---|
| *kale + ricotta ravioli* | | MA | | |
| *rosemary lentils with walnuts* | | MA | V | |
| *red wine + blueberry sorbet* | | MA | V | |

## WINE PAIRING

The Alpine vineyards of northern Italy's Alto Adige produce lovely Pinot Bianco, whose floral aromas and subtle beeswax flavors are positively delicious with a simple menu like this.

## COOKING ORDER

*1.* sorbet

*2.* ravioli

*3.* lentils

## WARDROBE CHANGE

Make the sorbet, prep the ravioli, and make the lentils. Change before boiling the ravioli. Or, if you want to make the ravioli with your partner, change before assembling and make the ravioli together.

TOTAL TIME: 1 1/2 HOURS / MAKES 20 RAVIOLI (6 PER PERSON + 8 LEFTOVER FOR LUNCH)

# kale + ricotta *ravioli*

1/2 bunch kale (about 1/2 pound), stems removed

1 clove garlic, minced

2 tablespoons extra virgin olive oil

1/2 teaspoon fine grain sea salt, plus more for pasta water

1/4 teaspoon freshly ground black pepper

1/4 cup breadcrumbs

1/4 cup ricotta

1/2 pound fresh lasagna sheets (see Note)

1 large egg, beaten

1 tablespoon unsalted butter

1 tablespoon chopped fresh sage leaves

2 tablespoons freshly grated Parmesan cheese

*continued*

## notes

**If you cannot get fresh lasagna sheets,** wonton wrappers could be used in a pinch. You can also use dry lasagna sheets and make the ravioli as sort of "deconstructed" ravioli by cooking the lasagna sheets, cutting them into squares, spooning the mixture onto them, laying another square on top and repeating. The affect is lasagna. If you do this, boil your lasagna, take out the sheets with tongs and use that boiling water to blanch the kale.

**Kale shrinks in volume** after blanching, making it easier to hold and chop.

**Store uncooked ravioli** in the freezer separated by parchment paper. Simply slip them off the parchment and into boiling salted water when you're ready to serve.

• Put a large pot of water over high heat to boil. Blanch the kale in boiling water for 1 minute. Drain, rinse with cold water, and let cool. Squeeze out as much water as you can with your hands. Finely chop the kale.

• Stir together the kale, garlic, 1 tablespoon olive oil, salt, and pepper in a bowl. Set aside 1/4 cup of this mixture. Add the breadcrumbs and ricotta to the bowl and stir until combined.

• Lay the lasagna sheets on a plate and cover with a moist dish cloth to keep pasta from drying out. Using a 3-inch round cookie cutter, cut rounds out of the pasta close together so as not to waste the dough.

• In the center of each round, place a teaspoon of the kale-ricotta filling. Rub a little egg around the rim of the circle with your finger and seal with another round, pressing firmly together around the rim, being careful not to puncture the dough. Repeat until the filling is gone (see photos, opposite page).

• Bring a large pot of salted water to a boil and cook the ravioli for 4 to 5 minutes. They should float when they are ready.

• Meanwhile, heat remaining 1 tablespoon of olive oil and the butter in a sauté pan over low heat. Add the sage and toast for 3 minutes. Add the reserved 1/4 cup kale and garlic mixture and cook for 2 minutes.

• Drain the ravioli and toss with sage sauce. Sprinkle with Parmesan before serving.

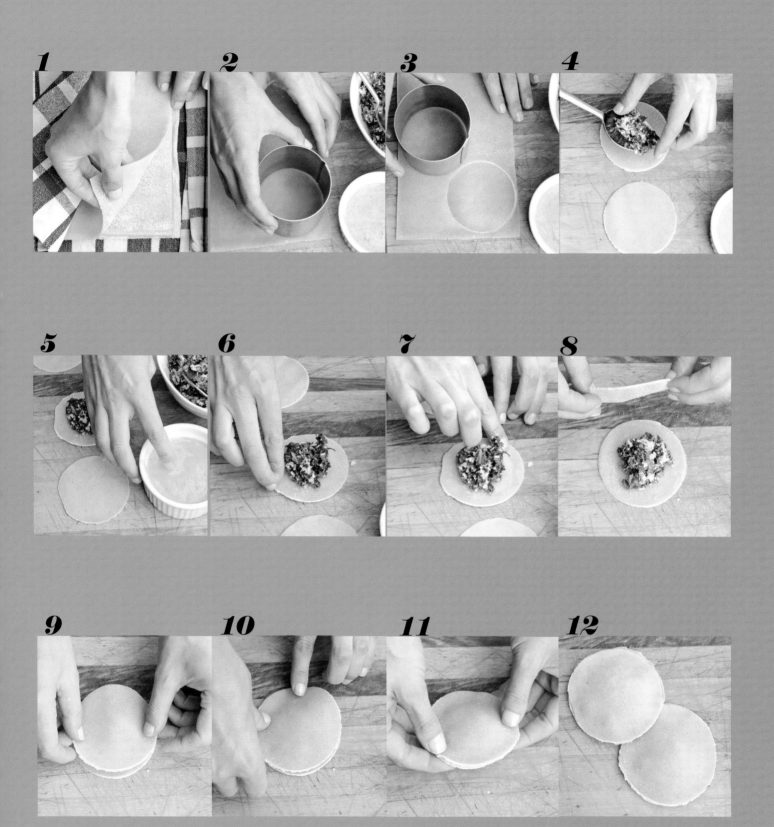

TOTAL TIME: 45 MINUTES / SERVES 2

MA V

# rosemary *lentils* with walnuts

**VINAIGRETTE:**

1/4 cup red wine vinegar

1 1/2 teaspoons chopped fresh rosemary

1 clove garlic, minced

2 tablespoons fine extra virgin olive oil

**LENTILS:**

1/3 cup dried French lentils

4 cups water

1 bay leaf

1/3 cup walnuts, chopped and toasted

1 scallion, chopped

1 cup quartered cherry tomatoes

2 tablespoons thinly sliced shallot (about 1 shallot)

1/4 teaspoon fine grain sea salt

Freshly ground black pepper

• MAKE THE VINAIGRETTE: In a bowl, whisk together the vinegar, rosemary, garlic, and olive oil. Set aside.

• PREPARE THE LENTILS: Put the lentils and 4 cups water in a pot over high heat; add the bay leaf. Boil until the lentils are soft, about 30 minutes. Strain; discard the bay leaf.

• While the lentils are warm, add the vinaigrette. Cool to room temperature.

• Stir in the walnuts, scallion, tomatoes, shallot, salt, and pepper to taste.

## notes

**French lentils** hold together firmly when cooked. Other lentils tend to get mushy if you don't watch out.

**Make the lentils one day in advance,** but don't add tomatoes or nuts until shortly before serving. Store covered in the refrigerator.

TOTAL TIME: 10 MINUTES PLUS FREEZING / SERVES 4

MA  V

# red wine + blueberry *sorbet*

1 cup red wine
1/4 cup turbinado or raw sugar
1 cup blueberries

• In a small nonreactive saucepan over medium heat, simmer the wine and sugar together until the sugar is dissolved.

• Transfer to a blender and add the berries. Blend until the berries break up but are not smooth.

• Freeze in a plastic container for at least 4 hours or use an ice cream machine according to manufacturer's instructions. To serve, scoop or scrape the sorbet into small bowls.

## notes

*Use any red wine* for this sorbet, but make sure it's good. It will determine the taste of the sorbet, and you'll be drinking the rest of it! We use Merlot.

*Try a sorbet duo* by using white wine and seedless green grapes for a second flavor!

*The sorbet be made in advance* and kept in the freezer for up to one month.

*last*

minute

*It always seems as though around six or seven at night*, a buddy will call: "What are you up to tonight?" When I realize that plans aren't going to make themselves, I usually dive into the waves head first and offer to have everyone over for a little dinner. I only have a moment to think before detouring to the market and slapping together a few stellar dishes—the ones that have given me the reputation of being a savvy hostess.

I love having people over, but my schedule is bonkers, so I am the queen of quick, last-minute dinners. I make popcorn or a quick dip with only a few ingredients and then make sure that everyone has a little wine. I am lucky to have a vino-genius friend in the business who always has the best recommendations (and whose recs are dotted throughout this book). That way, when guests come over, they have something to drink and nibble on without much effort from me. Read up on a few of these dishes now so you know what to pick up in a pinch! *xo,* Jill

# menu

| | SPEEDY | MAKE AHEAD | VEGAN | VEGAN FLEX |
|---|---|---|---|---|
| rosemary + olive oil popcorn | S | | V | |
| spicy saffron shrimp with yellow peppers | S | | | |
| potato kalamata pizza | S | | V | |
| chocolate black pepper cakes | S | | | |

## WINE PAIRING

Adventurous imbibers will delight in sipping a cool glass of manzanilla sherry with the popcorn before guzzling a Godello for the rest of the meal. This little-known Spanish grape variety was brought back from near extinction thanks to wines like Vina Godeval, whose fruit sap and mineral-flavored wine is hard to beat with seafood and saffron.

## COOKING ORDER

1. pizza
2. popcorn
3. shrimp
4. cakes

## WARDROBE CHANGE

Prep the cakes and then change. When your guests arrive, put the cakes in the oven. If you're really running short on time, save the popcorn for last and ask early guests to shake the pot while you make your change.

TOTAL TIME: 15 MINUTES / SERVES 8

S V

# rosemary + olive oil *popcorn*

2 tablespoons extra virgin olive oil

1 sprig fresh rosemary plus 4 teaspoons finely chopped

1/2 cup popcorn kernels

1/2 teaspoon fine grain sea salt

• In a large pot over medium-low heat, add the olive oil and rosemary sprig. Let the rosemary fry in the oil, 3 minutes, then remove the sprig.

Add the popcorn to the oil and cover the pot. Turn the heat to medium and pop the popcorn, shaking the pot every now and then to prevent kernels on the bottom from burning.

• When popcorn kernels have slowed popping, transfer to a serving bowl. Add the chopped rosemary and salt. Give the popcorn a shake and serve warm.

## notes

**For variety,** try this recipe with thyme or sage.

**You could also finish with** truffle salt and sugar, salt and cracked black pepper, or shichimi togarashi (see Party Extra, page 107).

TOTAL TIME: 25 MINUTES / SERVES 8

S

# spicy saffron *shrimp* with yellow peppers

*2 tablespoons extra virgin olive oil*

*2 shallots, chopped*

*1/4 teaspoon red chile pepper flakes*

*1/4 teaspoon saffron*

*3 yellow bell peppers, sliced into 1-inch batons*

*2 pounds (32 count) shrimp, peeled and butterflied*

• In a large sauté pan over medium heat, heat 2 tablespoons olive oil; sauté the shallots and chile flakes, 3 minutes. Add the saffron and cook for 2 minutes. Add the bell peppers and cook for 5 minutes. Add the shrimp and cook until pink, about 3 more minutes. Serve hot.

## notes

**If you're in a pinch** and can't find saffron, add two teaspoons of minced garlic for added flavor.

**This recipe also works** well with scallops or squid.

TOTAL TIME: 1 HOUR / SERVES 8

S V

# potato kalamata *pizza*

1 pound whole wheat pizza dough (see Note)

1 pound fingerling potatoes

3 tablespoons extra virgin olive oil

1/2 teaspoon fine grain sea salt

1 sprig fresh rosemary

3/4 cup kalamata or black olives, pitted

2 tablespoons chopped fresh flat-leaf parsley

1 tablespoon fine extra virgin olive oil, for drizzling

• Preheat the oven to 400°F. Roll the pizza dough into a circle about 14 inches in diameter with a rolling pin and place on a parchment-lined cookie sheet.

• Slice the potatoes 1/4 inch thick using a mandoline. Toss the potatoes with 2 tablespoons olive oil and the salt. Spread them out on a rimmed baking sheet and top with the rosemary sprig. Roast for 45 minutes, stirring halfway through.

• In a food processor, combine the olives with the remaining 1 tablespoon olive oil to make a quick tapenade. Pulse until mostly smooth.

• Spread the tapenade evenly over the pizza dough. Layer on the potatoes. Discard the rosemary.

• Reduce oven heat to 350°F and bake the pizza until the crust is browned, 10 to 12 minutes. Sprinkle with chopped parsley and drizzle with fine olive oil.

## notes

**Whole wheat pizza dough** can be purchased in many grocery stores. You can also check with your local pizzeria—they may be willing to sell uncooked dough. If you can't find whole wheat in a pinch, the next best thing is white pizza dough made with organic ingredients.

**Though we don't include cheese** on our pie, some people might like some shaved Parmesan or pecorino. Add them as soon as the pie comes out of the oven.

TOTAL TIME: 35 MINUTES / SERVES 8

S

# chocolate black pepper *cakes*

8 tablespoons (1 stick) unsalted butter, plus more for ramekins

4 large eggs

1/2 cup turbinado or raw sugar

12 ounces semisweet chocolate chips

4 teaspoons whole wheat pastry flour

1 teaspoon freshly ground black pepper

• Preheat the oven to 350°F. Butter 8 ovenproof ramekins.

• In a medium bowl, beat the eggs and sugar together with an electric mixer until fluffy, 5 minutes.

• Place the chocolate and butter in a microwave-safe bowl. Microwave on the defrost setting or 50% power for 30-second intervals until the chocolate is melted, 1 to 2 minutes total, stirring at each interval.

• Add the chocolate to the eggs, stirring to combine. Add the flour and the pepper; mix well. Pour into the ramekins.

• Bake for 25 minutes. The tops will have a hard shell and the centers should remain a little gooey.

## notes

**Yes, this is the same black pepper** that you grind onto your dinner plate. Be sure to use freshly ground here, too.

**These cakes should be served warm,** so put them in the oven after the party starts.

**Martha Stewart is the inspiration** for this dish. Her chocolate–black pepper cookies are Jill's favorite. This dessert reinvents those flavors.

# *menu*

| | SPEEDY | MAKE AHEAD | VEGAN | VEGAN FLEX |
|---|---|---|---|---|
| *tomato tartlets* | S | | | |
| *seared tofu + couscous salad* | S | MA | V | |
| *cumin-spiced carrots* | S | MA | V | |
| *fig truffles* | | MA | | VF |

## WINE PAIRING

A few splashes of Vermentino from Provence or Sardinia provide the perfect refreshment for this savory get-together. Keep a bottle of Armagnac on hand for those who want to add some spirit to the fig truffles.

## COOKING ORDER

*1.* truffles

*2.* carrots

*3.* salad

*4.* tartlets

## WARDROBE CHANGE

Make the truffles, carrots, and salad. Change once the tomatoes are roasting and the puff pastry is baking for the tartlets.

TOTAL TIME: 40 MINUTES / SERVES 8 TO 10

# tomato tartlets

6 Roma tomatoes

2 tablespoons extra virgin olive oil

1 tablespoon honey

1 tablespoon white balsamic vinegar (see Note)

1/2 teaspoon fine grain sea salt

1/2 teaspoon freshly ground black pepper

1 sheet puff pastry, thawed (see Note)

2 teaspoons minced fresh oregano

1 teaspoon fresh lemon juice

1 cup ricotta cheese

• Preheat the oven to 400°F. Slice the tomatoes into rounds (5 to 6 per tomato). Drizzle the tomatoes with olive oil, honey, vinegar, salt, and pepper. Toss until coated and transfer to a rimmed baking sheet. Roast for 30 minutes.

• Cut the puff pastry into 32 rectangles and place on a cookie sheet. Bake the puff pastry until golden and crisp, 8 to 10 minutes (you can pop it in with the tomatoes).

• Remove the puff pastry and tomatoes from oven. Let both cool slightly.

• In a small bowl, mix together the oregano, lemon juice, and ricotta. Smear each pastry square with this mixture and top with 1 to 2 tomato slices, browned side up.

## notes

**If you don't have white balsamic vinegar,** you can use regular balsamic.

**Alert! Alert! Remember to thaw out your puff pastry!** And, definitely try to get an all-butter puff pastry, like Dufour. It may be more expensive than the average, but it produces tastier, fuller results, and it's much better for your body than all those chemicals that are in many store-bought puff pastries.

TOTAL TIME: 50 MINUTES / SERVES 8 TO 10

# seared tofu + couscous *salad*

2 cups whole grain Israeli couscous

3 1/2 cups water

3 tablespoons extra virgin olive oil

2 pints cherry tomatoes, halved

2 teaspoons freshly ground black pepper

2 pounds extra-firm tofu (roughly 2 packages), patted dry and cut into 1-inch cubes

2 teaspoons curry powder

1 English cucumber, peeled and chopped

1 jalapeño, seeded and finely chopped

1/2 cup thinly sliced red onion

1 teaspoon grated lemon zest

1 tablespoon fresh mint leaves cut into a chiffonade

1/2 teaspoon fine grain sea salt

• Place the couscous in a dry skillet with a lid over medium heat and toast until it's brown, 5 to 6 minutes.

• In a large sauce pan, bring 3 1/2 cups water to a boil. Add the couscous, cover, and turn off the heat. Let sit for 15 minutes, then transfer the couscous to a large bowl.

• Return the skillet to medium heat and add 1 tablespoon olive oil. Add the tomatoes and sprinkle with 1/2 teaspoon pepper; sauté 5 minutes. Transfer to the bowl with the couscous and set aside.

• In the same skillet over medium heat, add 1 tablespoon olive oil. Add the tofu cubes and sprinkle with curry; sauté, flipping to crisp at least two sides, about 10 minutes. You may need to work the tofu in batches depending on the size of your pan. Set aside.

• Mix the cucumber, jalapeño, onion, zest, mint, and tofu with the tomatoes and couscous. Season with salt and the remaining pepper. Drizzle with the remaining 1 tablespoon olive oil.

## notes

**Don't know how to make a chiffonade?** See Quick Reference (page 256).

**Toasting the couscous** is key for adding depth of flavor to this recipe. You can buy toasted couscous, but we think it tastes better when we toast our own.

**You can make this in advance,** but don't add the cucumber until the day of the party. Store covered in the refrigerator.

TOTAL TIME: 45 MINUTES / SERVES 8

S MA V

# cumin-spiced *carrots*

2 pounds baby carrots

3 tablespoons extra virgin olive oil

2 teaspoons ground cumin

2 teaspoons freshly ground black pepper

3/4 teaspoon fine grain sea salt

• Preheat the oven to 400°F. Toss the carrots with the olive oil, cumin, pepper, and salt. Place on a rimmed baking sheet and roast until fork tender and browned, 30 to 40 minutes.

### notes

**The carrots can be made one day in advance.** Store covered in the refrigerator and reheat in a 350°F oven before serving.

**This dish requires almost no prep**—you don't even have to peel the carrots!

TOTAL TIME: 45 MINUTES INCLUDING COOLING / MAKES 10 TRUFFLES

MA VF

# fig truffles

1 cup semisweet chocolate chips

10 fresh green or black figs

1/2 cup shelled, crushed pistachios

• Place the chocolate in a microwave-safe bowl and microwave on the defrost setting or 50% power for 2 minutes. Stir the chocolate gently with a spoon and continue heating at 1 minute intervals, stirring after each minute, until the chocolate is thoroughly melted.

• Slice the tops off of the figs, making them as circular as possible. Dip the figs, one at a time, into the chocolate to coat and then roll them in the pistachios.

• Let set in the refrigerator for at least 30 minutes before serving.

## notes

**You can also do this with other fruits** if you can't find fresh figs. Try it with green grapes or even suprêmed orange slices.

**Truffles can be made one day in advance.** Store loosely covered in the fridge.

**Substitute with vegan chocolate** for a vegan dessert.

**These are much easier to make than traditional truffles** and have the plus of an explosive fig center.

*last-minute*

# menu

| | SPEEDY | MAKE AHEAD | VEGAN | VEGAN FLEX |
|---|---|---|---|---|
| *green salad with basil balsamic dressing* | S | MA | V | |
| *sea bass with tomato + olive gremolata* | S | | | |
| *warm quinoa, kale + goat cheese salad* | S | MA | | VF |
| *snowed-in berries* | S | | | |

## WINE PAIRING

Tangy tomatoes, goat cheese, and balsamic dressing require a wine with comparable crispness, so look for any of the Sauvignon Blanc–based wines of the Loire Valley: Sancerre, Quincy, Pouilly-Fumé, and Menetou-Salon are all worthy companions.

## COOKING ORDER

**1.** quinoa salad

**2.** sea bass

**3.** green salad

**4.** berries

## WARDROBE CHANGE

Make everything except the berries and change. Bake the berries after guests arrive—they taste best straight from the oven. Since this menu is quick, you should even have time to shower!

TOTAL TIME: 15 MINUTES / SERVES 10

S MA V

# *green salad*
## *with basil balsamic dressing*

**DRESSING:**

*1/2 cup balsamic vinegar*

*1/2 cup extra virgin olive oil*

*1/3 cup fresh basil leaves, packed*

*2 tablespoons Dijon mustard*

*1/4 teaspoon fine grain sea salt*

*1/4 teaspoon freshly ground black pepper*

*8 cups tender greens, your choice*

• MAKE THE DRESSING: Blend everything together in a blender.

• Pour 1/4 cup dressing over greens and toss. Serve the remaining dressing on the side for guests to add if they want more.

*notes*

**The dressing will keep** for one week; store covered in the refrigerator.

**This makes enough dressing** for quick lunches, too: Use it in another salad or use it as a spread on a roasted vegetable sandwich.

TOTAL TIME: 60 MINUTES / SERVES 8

S

# sea bass
## with roasted tomato + olive gremolata

1 pint cherry tomatoes, halved

2 tablespoons extra virgin olive oil

10 kalamata olives, pitted and quartered

1/4 cup roughly chopped fresh flat-leaf parsley

1 teaspoon grated lemon zest

2 cloves garlic, minced

4 sea bass fillets, halved (3 pounds) (see Note)

1/2 teaspoon fine grain sea salt

1/2 teaspoon freshly ground black pepper

• Preheat the oven to 400°F. Toss the tomatoes in olive oil. Spread out on a rimmed baking sheet and roast in the oven until the tomatoes are wilted, about 15 minutes. Remove from oven and set aside.

• Mix together the olives, parsley, lemon zest, and garlic.

• Reduce the oven temperature to 350°F. Place the fish skin side up on a parchment-lined, rimmed baking sheet; sprinkle with salt and pepper. Bake until fish is opaque and flakes easily, about 20 minutes.

• Combine the tomatoes with the olive mixture.

• Remove the fish from the oven and serve topped with the gremolata.

### notes

**Striped bass, Chilean bass, or any fish,** actually, goes well with the gremolata. Just pick up the fish that looks freshest to you from the most ethical fishmonger you can find.

TOTAL TIME: 30 MINUTES / SERVES 8

# *warm quinoa, kale + goat cheese* **salad**

2 cups quinoa

4 cups water

1/4 cup extra virgin olive oil

10 cloves garlic, minced

2 bunches kale (about 2 pounds), ribs removed, chopped

1/2 teaspoon fine grain sea salt

2 tablespoons fresh lemon juice (from about 1 lemon)

1 teaspoon grated lemon zest

1/2 teaspoon freshly ground black pepper

4 ounces fresh goat cheese, crumbled

• Place the quinoa in a medium saucepan over medium-high heat without any oil. Toast, stirring, until the color deepens, about 5 minutes. Add the water and reduce the heat to low. Let the quinoa simmer, covered, until all the water is absorbed, about 15 minutes.

• Meanwhile, place your largest sauté pan over low heat. Add the olive oil and sauté the garlic until fragrant and lightly browned, 3 to 4 minutes. Add the kale and salt and sauté until the kale is cooked and wilted, about 10 minutes.

• Mix together the quinoa and kale. Add the lemon juice, zest, and pepper. Top with the goat cheese.

### *notes*

***Quinoa*** comes in tan, red, and black. The red and black varieties have a nuttier taste. Use whichever you prefer.

***You can make the salad one day in advance,*** but leave the goat cheese aside until it's time to serve. Store covered in the refrigerator.

***To make this a vegan dish,*** omit the goat cheese.

TOTAL TIME: 35 MINUTES / SERVES 8

- - - - - - - - - - - - - - - - - - - - - - - - - - - - - - - - - - - - - - - - - - - - - - - - - - - - - - - - S

# snowed-in *berries*

2 cups blackberries

2 cups blueberries

2 tablespoons fresh lemon juice (from about 1 lemon)

1/2 cup turbinado or raw sugar

3 egg whites

1/4 teaspoon cream of tartar

1/2 teaspoon grated lemon zest

• Preheat the oven to 325°F. In a nonreactive bowl, mix the berries, lemon juice, and 1/4 cup sugar. Place in an 8x8-inch baking dish. You can also divide this among 8 individual ramekins.

• Using an electric mixer, in a clean bowl, beat the egg whites with cream of tartar until soft peaks form, 3 to 4 minutes. Slowly beat in the remaining 1/4 cup sugar and lemon zest and continue beating until the meringue is a little stiff, about 2 to 3 minutes.

• Pour the fluffy meringue over the berries. Bake until the meringue begins to brown, about 15 minutes.

## notes

***Get your berries ready before dinner.*** When clearing the dishes, whip up the meringue and pop it in the oven. It's ready after fifteen minutes and most glorious when served right from the oven.

blowout

*parties*

*We love big events!* We unabashedly plan the menu, pick out flowers, obsess over a playlist, rip ideas from *Elle Décor*, get midnight inspiration that derails the whole theme, then replan from scratch, and invite everyone we know! These bashes aren't for every day, so when the opportunity arises, it feels great to get it right. Jump into planning your big party wholeheartedly, and your reward will be smiling, satiated friends. Even if the weather doesn't cooperate, having great food somehow provides invincibility to any occasion. We once had a rooftop birthday party in August that was saved from torrential rain showers by black bean, avocado, and corn tacos, a mocha chocolate cake, and a delicious Lillet-spiked punch (page 251). After seeing the photos, no-shows intimidated by the weather still regret that they didn't come! *xo, Jill & Josie*

# *menu*

| | SPEEDY | MAKE AHEAD | VEGAN | VEGAN FLEX |
|---|---|---|---|---|
| *cheese plate with spiced kumquat jam* | | MA | | |
| *chicken + apricot falafel* | | MA | | |
| *spicy lemon + date chutney with warm pita* | | MA | V | |
| *herbed goat cheese toasts with salmon roe* | S | MA | | |

## WINE PAIRING

Any blowout worth your time deserves almost as many elixirs as amuse. Magnum bottles of bubbly and Beaujolais-Villages are festive, food-friendly, and delicious, but don't forget the sake—a good poke should be washed down with a cool glass of Junmai or Ginjo. Use a good one when making the Twinkle Toes, and serve the rest straight up.

## COOKING ORDER

We don't expect you to make everything! However, no matter your selects, strive to do the "Make Ahead" items first.

## WARDROBE CHANGE

Prep it all and get dressed when only the delicate steps of plating and garnishing remain. Wear an apron while you replenish any plates; it's never a bad thing to let guests know who's responsible for all the food they've been gobbling up!

|                                      | SPEEDY | MAKE AHEAD | VEGAN | VEGAN FLEX |
| ------------------------------------ | ------ | ---------- | ----- | ---------- |
| *shrimp cocktail*                    |        | MA         |       |            |
| *sweet pea + zucchini cakes*         |        |            |       |            |
| *tuna poke*                          |        |            |       |            |
| *chorizo red pepper polenta squares* |        | MA         |       | VF         |
| *lavender shortbread cookies*        |        | MA         |       |            |
| *chocolate chip cookies*             |        | MA         |       |            |
| *grapefruit blackberry flirt*        |        |            | V     |            |
| *twinkle toes*                       |        |            | V     |            |

# cheese plate
## with spiced kumquat jam

Cheese platters are a familiar party staple that guests love. They are easy to make and can be ready to go while you're finishing up the last bits of other dishes. For an enticing cheese platter, keep these things in mind:

• *Have a selection of at least three cheeses*—about one ounce per person, per type of cheese. For example, with three types of cheese for a ten-person party, that's about two pounds of cheese.

• *A theme of cheeses often works.* You could select a variety of goat cheeses, cheeses from the same region, or locally crafted cheeses. You could also select cheeses made from different milks—cow, sheep, goat, etc.

• *Be sure to vary the selection* in terms of texture and pungency. If you are working within a theme, keep the cheeses different enough so that guests with varying tastes have options.

• *Serve your cheese* with crackers, fruits, nuts, or vegetables with which your guests may sample the cheeses. A sweet and complex spread, like the kumquat jam, will play off the salty notes of each cheese without overpowering its flavor.

• *When laying out your cheeses,* be sure to leave enough space for guests to be able to slice one cheese without ruining the rest of the platter. You may also decide to preslice harder cheeses and arrange them neatly.

• *It's a good idea to select cheeses that pair well* with wines being served at your party. Ask your cheesemonger or the cutie at the wine shop for help.

*211*

BLOWOUT PARTIES

TOTAL TIME: 45 MINUTES / SERVES 10

# spiced kumquat *jam*

1 cup water

4 allspice berries

1 star anise

1 cinnamon stick

1 pint fresh kumquats, each sliced into 4 rings

3/4 cup turbinado or raw sugar

• Simmer everything together in a nonreactive pot over low heat, 30 minutes, stirring once or twice. Let the jam cool to room temperature. Remove the spices before serving.

*notes*

**Dried or candied kumquats** are fine, but omit the sugar. This jam pairs well with the saltiness of cheese.

**This can be made** one day in advance; store covered in the refrigerator.

TOTAL TIME: 50 MINUTES / SERVES 8 TO 10 (MAKES 20 FALAFEL)

# chicken + apricot *falafel*

**SAUCE:**

1/4 cup fresh lemon juice (from about 2 lemons)

4 teaspoons grated lemon zest

1/4 cup tahini

1/2 cup cooked chickpeas

1/2 cup water

1 clove garlic

1 teaspoon red chile pepper flakes

**FALAFEL:**

1 cup dried apricots (about 6 ounces)

1 cup cooked chickpeas

2 cloves garlic

1/2 cup roughly chopped fresh cilantro

1/2 cup roughly chopped fresh flat-leaf parsley

4 scallions, roughly chopped

1 teaspoon ground cumin

1 teaspoon red chile pepper flakes

1 teaspoon ground coriander

1/2 teaspoon fine grain sea salt

1/4 teaspoon freshly ground black pepper

1 pound ground chicken (dark meat)

• Preheat the oven to 400°F. Line a rimmed baking sheet with parchment paper.

• MAKE THE SAUCE: Put the lemon juice, zest, tahini, chickpeas, water, garlic, and chile flakes in a blender or food processor and purée until super smooth. Set the sauce aside.

• MAKE THE FALAFEL: Place all the ingredients except the chicken in a food processor and blend until chunky. Using a spoon, mix in the chicken. Let sit for 10 minutes. Form into 1-inch balls with moistened hands. Place on the prepared baking sheet and bake until chicken is cooked all the way through, about 20 minutes.

• Serve hot with the sauce as a dip.

MA

## notes

*Tahini,* a sesame seed paste, is usually found near the olives and other Mediterranean goods at your grocery.

*For tips on cooking chickpeas* see Quick Reference (page 257).

*Dark meat* (from the leg and thigh) is key for this recipe; it keeps the falafel moist. Look for it with the other ground meats. You can use white meat if that's all you can find, but your falafel might be very dry.

*The sauce can be made* one day in advance; store covered in the refrigerator.

TOTAL TIME: 60 MINUTES / SERVES 10

# spicy lemon + date *chutney* with warm pita

2 1/2 cups pitted, chopped dates

1/2 cup fresh lemon juice (from about 4 lemons)

2 cups water

1 teaspoon ground cumin

2 tablespoons grated fresh ginger

1 teaspoon crushed red chile pepper flakes

1 teaspoon fine grain sea salt

1 package whole wheat pita bread

Extra virgin olive oil

• Place a medium-size saucepan over medium heat and add the dates, lemon juice, water, cumin, ginger, chile flakes, and salt. Simmer until the water is almost gone, about 30 minutes.

• Purée the chutney in a food processor or with an immersion blender until fairly smooth. Let cool.

• To serve, preheat the oven to 350°F. Cut each pita into 8 triangles, place on a baking sheet, and drizzle with olive oil. Toast them in the oven for 4 to 7 minutes. Serve the chutney as a dip for the warm, crisped pita.

## notes

*The chutney can be made* one day in advance; store covered in the refrigerator.

*Definitely make extra*—you can use the chutney on a sandwich the following day.

TOTAL TIME: 20 MINUTES / SERVES 6 TO 8

# herbed goat cheese *toasts* with salmon roe

4 slices whole grain bread, crusts trimmed

Olive oil cooking spray

8 ounces fresh goat cheese

3 tablespoons finely chopped chives

1 teaspoon sumac

2 teaspoons grated lemon zest

2 teaspoons fresh lemon juice (from about 1/2 lemon)

2 ounces salmon roe

Chervil leaves, for garnish (optional)

• Preheat the oven to 400°F. Cut the bread into bite-size triangles. Place on a baking sheet, spray with olive oil, and toast for 5 minutes in the oven. Let cool.

• Meanwhile, mix the goat cheese, chives, sumac, lemon zest, and juice together. Smear the toasts with goat cheese and top each with 1 teaspoon roe. Garnish with chervil leaves, if using.

## notes

**You can season** the goat cheese several hours before serving time; store in the refrigerator until ready to use.

**Sumac?** Like poison sumac?? No, no, we're talking about the tart, ground spice that Middle Easterners use to add depth of flavor to many of their dishes. It adds a tart, almost citrus note.

**Salmon roe** and salmon caviar are the same.

TOTAL TIME: 45 MINUTES / SERVES 10

# shrimp cocktail

2 pounds (24-count) shrimp

4 quarts water

2 cups white wine

14 black peppercorns

3 lemons, sliced 1/4-inch thin

1/4 whole vanilla bean

6 sprigs fresh tarragon

1 teaspoon fine grain sea salt

**COCKTAIL SAUCE:**

1 cup ketchup

2 tablespoons fresh lemon juice
(from about 1 lemon)

2 teaspoons grated lemon zest

1/3 cup prepared horseradish

• Peel and devein the shrimp. Set aside in the fridge.

• In a large pot over medium heat, simmer the water, wine, peppercorns, lemons, vanilla, tarragon, and salt for 30 minutes. Remove from heat and strain the liquid into another pot. Add the shrimp and let sit for 20 minutes, as the liquid cools down. Discard the spices.

• MEANWHILE, MAKE THE COCKTAIL SAUCE: Combine the ketchup with lemon juice, zest, and horseradish.

• Drain the shrimp and let it cool in the fridge. Serve with the cocktail sauce on the side.

*notes*

**The shrimp can be made** a few hours in advance; keep chilled.

**The sauce can be made** one day in advance; store covered in the refrigerator.

**The court bouillon,** or broth, transforms this from standard cocktail fare to outstanding.

TOTAL TIME: 50 MINUTES / SERVES 8 (MAKES 32 CAKES)

# *sweet pea + zucchini* **cakes**

1 zucchini

1 teaspoon fine grain sea salt

1 1/2 cups fresh shucked peas, or frozen and thawed

1 tablespoon chopped fresh mint leaves, packed

1/4 cup milk

1 large egg

1/2 cup whole wheat pastry flour

1/2 teaspoon baking powder

2 tablespoons unsalted butter

1/4 cup crème fraîche

2 chives, chopped

• Shred the zucchini with the small julienne blade of a mandoline or cheese grater. Place the zucchini in a strainer over a bowl and mix with 1/2 teaspoon salt. Let the moisture drain out for 20 minutes. Rinse the zucchini and squeeze the water out of it. It should yield about 1/2 cup of zucchini.

• Blend the peas, the remaining 1/2 teaspoon salt, and the mint in a food processor until smooth. Add the milk and egg and pulse for 15 seconds.

• In a small bowl, mix together the flour and baking powder. Add the flour mixture to the food processor with the pea mixture and pulse for another 10 seconds.

• In a large bowl, mix together the pea mixture and the strained zucchini.

• Heat 1 tablespoon butter in a skillet over medium heat. Drop tablespoonfuls of the batter into the pan and brown on both sides, 3 to 5 minutes per side. Place the cooked cakes on a wire rack while you make the next batch. Add another tablespoon of butter to the pan and cook the remaining batter.

• Serve the cooled cakes topped with crème fraîche and chives.

*notes*

*These delicate pancakes* don't like to wait to be eaten, so try not to make them more than two hours in advance.

TOTAL TIME: 20 MINUTES PLUS MARINATING / SERVES 6 TO 8

# *tuna poke*

1/4 cup chopped Thai basil leaves

1 teaspoon minced fresh ginger

1 jalapeño, seeded and chopped

1 scallion, chopped

2 cloves garlic, minced

1/4 cup low-sodium soy sauce

1 teaspoon hot chili sauce, such as Sriracha

2 teaspoons sesame oil

1/2 pound fresh sushi-grade tuna, cut into 1/2-inch cubes

1/2 seedless cucumber, peeled, quartered, and sliced

20 brown rice crackers

• In a bowl, whisk together the Thai basil, ginger, jalapeño, scallion, garlic, soy sauce, hot sauce, and sesame oil until thoroughly combined. Mix in the tuna and cucumbers and chill for 2 to 3 hours.

• Serve on top of rice crackers.

## *notes*

*Poke* (pronounced "POH-kay") originates from Hawaii, so imagine eating it with cool surf and fragrant tropical flowers as your backdrop.

*If you can't find Thai basil,* use a mix of half regular basil and half mint for a similar effect.

TOTAL TIME: 1 HOUR, 15 MINUTES / SERVES 10 (MAKES 64 SQUARES)

# chorizo red pepper *polenta* squares

1 (8-ounce) fresh chorizo
sausage

1 yellow onion, chopped

1 red bell pepper, diced

2 teaspoons extra virgin olive
oil

1/2 teaspoon fine grain sea salt

2 1/2 cups water

1 cup quick-cook polenta

Olive oil cooking spray

• Take the chorizo out of the casing. In a large saucepan over medium-high heat, brown the chorizo, stirring and breaking it up, until cooked, about 5 minutes. Add the onion, bell pepper, olive oil, and salt, and continue sautéing until the onion is soft, about 6 minutes.

• Add the water and bring to a simmer. Whisk in the polenta. Simmer, stirring, until the polenta is thick, about 1 minute. Remove from heat.

• Spray an 8x8-inch pan with olive oil. Pour the polenta evenly into the pan, smoothing out the top, and refrigerate, covered, for 15 minutes or until you're ready to serve. It will firm up as it cools.

• Preheat the broiler. Line a rimmed baking sheet with parchment paper. Cut the polenta into 1-inch squares and place on the baking sheet, leaving space between the squares. Spray the squares with olive oil and broil until crispy, about 2 minutes. Remove the baking sheet and flip the squares. Broil until crispy, about 2 more minutes.

## notes

*Dried chorizo sausage* can also be used; it will result in a stronger, saltier taste that's not for everyone.

*Omit the chorizo and substitute* smoked tofu or portabello mushrooms for a vegan dish. Simply dice and sauté.

*See Note on page 32* for more info on the different varieties of polenta.

TOTAL TIME: 2 HOURS / MAKES 80 COOKIES

MA

# lavender shortbread *cookies*

1 tablespoon dried lavender flowers

1/3 cup plus 1 tablespoon turbinado or raw sugar

1 cup (2 sticks) unsalted butter, at room temperature

2 1/2 cups whole wheat pastry flour

1/4 teaspoon fine grain sea salt

6 ounces white chocolate chips (about 1 cup)

• Pulse the lavender in a food processor with 1 tablespoon sugar.

• In a large bowl, use an electric mixer to beat the butter, lavender sugar, and 1/2 cup sugar until fluffy, about 5 minutes.

• In another bowl, combine the flour and salt. Stir the flour mixture into the butter mixture until combined. Roll the dough into a ball and flatten. Wrap in plastic wrap and chill in the refrigerator for 30 minutes.

• Preheat the oven to 350°F. Remove the dough from the refrigerator and place it on parchment paper or a floured surface; roll out to 1/4-inch thickness. Slice into 1-inch squares. Lay the squares 1 inch apart on a cookie sheet, cover, and refrigerate for another 20 minutes.

• Uncover the cookies and bake them until slightly firm, 18 to 20 minutes. Remove cookies to wire racks to cool.

• Place the chocolate in a microwave-safe bowl and microwave on the defrost setting or 50% power for 1 minute. Stir the chocolate gently with a spoon and continue heating at 1 minute intervals, stirring after each minute, until the chocolate is thoroughly melted.

• When the cookies are cool, dip one corner of each cookie into the white chocolate and lay on a parchment sheet 1 inch apart. Let the white chocolate cool to harden. If your kitchen is hot, you may need to let the chocolate-dipped cookies chill in the fridge so the chocolate has a chance to harden.

## notes

*For added glamour,* dust the white chocolate with purple sanding sugar or candied violets before it dries. Or, drizzle the white chocolate in stripes across the cookie.

*You can make these cookies* two to three days in advance, just store them separated by wax or parchment paper in an airtight container.

TOTAL TIME: 2 HOURS, 45 MINUTES INCLUDING CHILLING / MAKES 50 TO 60 BITE-SIZE COOKIES

MA

# *chocolate chip* **cookies**

3/4 cup rolled oats

1/2 cup whole wheat pastry flour

1/4 teaspoon baking soda

1/2 teaspoon baking powder

1/4 teaspoon fine grain sea salt

1/4 cup coconut oil

1/3 cup turbinado or raw sugar

1/2 cup dark brown sugar, packed

1 large egg

1 teaspoon pure vanilla extract

1 1/2 cups semisweet chocolate chips

Flaky sea salt, such as Maldon

• Blend the oats in a food processor until floury. Add the flour, baking soda, baking powder, and salt to the food processor and pulse until combined, about 20 seconds.

• Cream the coconut oil, raw sugar, brown sugar, egg, and vanilla with a electric mixer on high speed for 3 minutes. Stir the flour mixture into the wet ingredients. Stir in the chocolate chips. Let the dough rest in the freezer for 2 hours.

• Place a rack in the middle of the oven and preheat the oven to 325°F. Form the dough into marble-size balls and lay them on a parchment-lined cookie sheet about 1 inch apart. Sprinkle with a little flaked salt. Bake on the middle rack until cookies are just firm, about 8 minutes. Remove the cookies to a wire rack to cool; they will harden further.

## notes

**Make sure you beat** the coconut oil and sugar together for the full 3 minutes. If you don't, you may get flat, crisp cookies.

**These cookies can be made** a day or two in advance. Store in an airtight container.

TOTAL TIME: 10 MINUTES / SERVES 6

# grapefruit blackberry *flirt*

18 blackberries

1 cup freshly squeezed grapefruit juice

3 cups Prosecco

• Smash 12 blackberries through a strainer to yield 3 tablespoons of juice. Distribute the juice evenly among 6 champagne flutes.

• Pour the grapefruit juice equally into the flutes, then top with Prosecco. Drop the remaining blackberries into each glass.

TOTAL TIME: 10 MINUTES PLUS MARINATING / SERVES 6

# *twinkle toes*

30 paper-thin cucumber slices

6 fresh basil leaves cut into a chiffonade

3 cups sake

Ice

1 1/2 cups club soda

• Place the cucumber slices, basil, and sake into a container and cover. Let marinate for at least 30 minutes.

• To serve, place 2 ice cubes each in 6 rocks glasses. Pour the sake into the glasses and top each with 1/4 cup soda.

## notes

**Don't know how to make a chiffonade?** See Quick Reference (page 256).

**Add a pinch** of food-grade gold dust to our Twinkle Toes. You can find it in a cake-decorating store. It will make your drinks twinkle!

# *menu*

| | SPEEDY | MAKE AHEAD | VEGAN | VEGAN FLEX |
|---|---|---|---|---|
| *yellow tomato gazpacho shooters* | S | MA | V | |
| *bean + grain burgers* | | | | VF |
| *sautéed mushrooms* | S | MA | V | |
| *mango relish* | S | MA | V | |
| *caramelized onions* | | MA | V | |

### WINE PAIRING

Amazingly quaffable South African Chenin Blanc can be found for between $8 and $15 per bottle, and when your blowout aims to combine flavors from around the globe, it's hard to find a more versatile wine for the price. Bargain hunters will enjoy bottlings from Man Vintners, but don't miss wines from Bruwer Raats, the MAN when it comes to Cape Chenin Blanc.

### COOKING ORDER

We don't expect you to make everything! However, no matter your selects, strive to do the "Make Ahead" items first.

### WARDROBE CHANGE

Prepare all of the bases here, but dress for grilling: Most of the cooking is done at the 'cue. Play the hostess in the rough—it's a BBQ after all!

|  | SPEEDY | MAKE AHEAD | VEGAN | VEGAN FLEX |
|---|---|---|---|---|
| cherry tomato chutney | | MA | V | |
| chimichurri marinade | S | MA | V | |
| garlic bbq sauce | | MA | V | |
| sweet chile marinade | S | MA | V | |
| "the colonel" spice mix | S | MA | V | |
| chili pop spice mix | S | MA | V | |
| lime of my life spice mix | S | MA | V | |
| chickpea peppadew salad | | MA | V | |
| grilled corn with avocado crema | | MA | V | |
| fingerling potato salad with celery leaves | | MA | V | |
| grilled grapefruit | S | | V | |
| pucker punch | | MA | V | |

BANGIN'CUE

# *grill guide*

A decent barbecue requires some basic things: a grill setup, foods to grill, a good variety of sides, and people to help cook and enjoy the food. Whether you have a charcoal or gas grill, it is helpful to have one large enough that it won't take all day to cook the items you plan on preparing. Set up "zones" on your grill, since generally one side should be much hotter than the other side. This serves a dual purpose: Different foods cook at different temperatures, so you'll always have a side ready to cook practically anything. And, if you notice something is cooking a little too fast (its exterior is burning while the inside is still raw) you can nudge it over to the cooler side.

### EQUIPMENT

• For charcoal grills: Soaked wood chips, if you're using them; charcoal, matches, and lighter fluid

• Platters for uncooked items: Keep vegetables and fruit separate from raw meats; raw meats should be stored in containers or tightly sealed plastic bags; lay the containers in a cooler with lots of ice

• Platters for cooked items

• A long-handled set of tongs and a long-handled spatula

• A grill basket for tiny pieces of food or whole fish (things that are harder to maneuver and flip)

BANGIN'CUE

# *grill guide*

### PREPARING TO GRILL

After you've selected what you want to grill, prep the food accordingly. Trim down and marinate meats, trim vegetables and slice them, make burger patties, clean shrimp, etc. Never reuse a marinade that meat has been marinating in already. Don't save it, serve it, or brush down cooked meat with it.

The grilling chart that follows is a general map for grilling various items. Grill temperatures range from low to high. Low is 250°F. High is around 500°F. If you don't have a grill thermometer, here's how you can gauge the temp: at low you can hold your hand roughly three inches over the grill for five or six seconds; at high you can hold it there for one second.

Apply the seasonings and sauces as suggested in the guide. Garlic Barbecue Sauce and Chimichurri can be served at the table as a condiment for the meat in addition to using them to brush onto grill items.

Prepare any salads and condiments that will accompany your grill items. Be sure to keep these cold. As with any party, have beverages and appetizers ready for guests to eat as they arrive. Our gazpacho can be made a few hours or one day in advance specifically for this purpose. And the Pucker Punch is better after a day of steeping, so get on it early.

Patience is key in grilling. Be sure to keep an eye on your food to avoid burning and flare-ups.

BANGIN'CUE

# grill guide

| Non-meat | Temperature | Seasoning options | Some helpful tips |
|----------|-------------|-------------------|-------------------|
| **VEGETABLES** | | Season vegetables just before grilling. Drizzle with a little olive oil and sprinkle on some spice. Or toss with sauce five minutes before grilling. | Vegetables are grilled until they are tender with a good char on them. |
| Leafy vegetables (radicchio, escarole) | medium-high | Lime of My Life, Chili Pop, Chimichurri | When prepping the vegetable, chop the bunch or head vertically once or twice, leaving the leaves attached to their stems. |
| Juicy vegetables (tomatoes) | medium-high | Lime of My Life, Chili Pop, Chimichurri | Halve the vegetable and grill skin side down. Do not turn. |
| Larger, firm vegetables (potatoes, zucchini, eggplant, bell peppers) | medium-high | Lime of My Life, "The Colonel," Chili Pop, Chimichurri, Garlic BBQ Sauce, Sweet Chile Marinade, balsamic marinade (see page 82) | Slice them about 1/4- to 1/2-inch thick for manageable grilling. They are done when tender. |
| Small, firm vegetables (mushrooms, cippolini onions, radishes, broccoli florets) | medium-high | Lime of My Life, Chili Pop, Chimichurri, Garlic BBQ Sauce, Sweet Chile Marinade | Can be grilled whole. Use a grill basket for easier handling. |
| Skinny vegetables (asparagus, green beans) | medium-high | Lime of My Life, "The Colonel," Chili Pop, Chimichurri | Lay foil over the grill to prevent them from falling between the cracks, or use a grill basket. |
| **BREAD** | medium | Lime of My Life, "The Colonel," Chili Pop | Slice the bread into the desired thickness. Spray both sides with olive oil and grill until marks appear. Flip and grill the other side until marks appear. |

BANGIN'CUE

# *grill guide*

| Non-meat | Temperature | Seasoning options | Some helpful tips |
|---|---|---|---|
| **FRUIT** | | | Depending on the fruit, you might want to keep the peel on, even if it is inedible. This gives you something firm to hold onto when you need to pick up the fruit. |
| Bananas | medium-low | Lime of My Life, Chili Pop, brown sugar and butter, cinnamon | Slice the banana peel from top to bottom. Open the peel, add spices, reseal. Grill the banana until the peel is a toasty brown. |
| Citrus fruit | medium-low | Lime of My Life, Chili Pop, Sweet Chile Marinade, brown sugar or agave syrup with salt | Cut into large wedges with peel, or halve the fruit and grill flesh side down. |
| Berries | medium | Lime of My Life, balsamic marinade (page 82) | Generally, grilling berries is not a great idea, with the exception of larger strawberries. |
| Stone fruit | medium-low | Lime of My Life, Chili Pop, Garlic BBQ Sauce, Sweet Chile Marinade | Slice the fruit in half and remove the pit. Cherries are not suitable for grilling. |
| Mangos, pineapple | medium-high | Lime of My Life, Chili Pop, Garlic BBQ Sauce, Sweet Chile Marinade, curry powder, smoked paprika | Cut the fruit into thick slices. |
| Melons | medium-high | Lime of My Life, Chili Pop, curry powder | Cut the fruit into thick slices. |
| **TOFU** | medium-high | Lime of My Life, "The Colonel," Chili Pop, Chimichurri, Garlic BBQ Sauce, Sweet Chile Marinade | Use extra-firm tofu. Drain the tofu first and oil both sides for better grill marks. |
| **VEGETARIAN BURGERS** | medium | Lime of My Life, "The Colonel," Chili Pop, Chimichurri, Garlic BBQ Sauce | Veggie burgers tend to fall apart easily, so be sure to oil your grill well and only turn once. You can sprinkle the spices right on top of the preformed, precooked burger. |

BANGIN'CUE

# BBQ grill guide

| Meats + Fish | Temperature | Seasoning options | Some helpful tips |
|---|---|---|---|
| **BONELESS CUTS** | | Dry spices can quickly season meat before cooking. Use Sweet Chile Marinade or a balsamic marinade for juicier grilling. It's best to let meats marinate for at least two hours. | Pat meats dry of any marinades before grilling. Butterflied and pounded pieces cook much faster. |
| Chicken breast | medium | Lime of My Life, "The Colonel," Chili Pop, Chimichurri, Garlic BBQ Sauce, Sweet Chile Marinade, balsamic marinade (see page 82) | Use a thermometer to check for doneness (165°F). |
| Fillets of beef | medium | Lime of My Life, Chili Pop, Chimichurri, Garlic BBQ Sauce, Sweet Chile Marinade, balsamic marinade (see page 82) | Use more tender cuts of beef for better results. Be sure to trim away most of the fat and connective tissue. |
| Fish fillets | medium-high | Lime of My Life, "The Colonel," Chili Pop, Chimichurri, Garlic BBQ Sauce, Sweet Chile Marinade, balsamic marinade (see page 82) | Use firm-fleshed fish, such as halibut, salmon, or tuna. Be sure your grill and fish are well oiled. Do not force the fish off of the grill. It is ready to flip when it lifts easily. It may be easier to grill skin side down. |
| Shrimp, lobster, soft-shell crab | medium-high | Lime of My Life, Chili Pop, Chimichurri, Garlic BBQ Sauce, Sweet Chile Marinade, balsamic marinade (see page 82) | Shrimp taste better when grilled with the shell on. It's harder to eat because you have to peel it, but that may be a good thing if you want to slow down the pace of the barbecue. |
| Sausages and hot dogs | medium | Chimichurri, Garlic BBQ Sauce | |
| Burgers | medium | Lime of My Life, "The Colonel," Chili Pop, Chimichurri, Garlic BBQ Sauce | |

BANGIN'CUE

# BBQ grill guide

| Meats + Fish | Temperature | Seasoning options | Some helpful tips |
|---|---|---|---|
| **BONE-IN CUTS** | | | Anything with bones is going to take much longer to cook. You don't want the flesh to dry out while the area near the bone is still undercooked. Marinades and low-temperature grilling help prevent this. Pat meats dry of any marinades before grilling. Close the grill for even cooking. |
| Ribs | low | Lime of My Life, "The Colonel," Chili Pop, Chimichurri, Garlic BBQ Sauce, Sweet Chile Marinade | Grill the meat for at least an hour with a dry spice rub. Then baste it with sauce for an additional ten minutes or so. |
| Pork chops | medium-low | Lime of My Life, "The Colonel," Chili Pop, Chimichurri, Garlic BBQ Sauce, Sweet Chile Marinade, balsamic marinade (see page 82) | Use a brine or marinade for tender chops. |
| Chicken parts | medium-low | Lime of My Life, "The Colonel," Chili Pop, Chimichurri, Garlic BBQ Sauce, Sweet Chile Marinade, balsamic marinade (see page 82) | Grill with or without the skin. |
| Whole fish | medium-low | Lime of My Life, "The Colonel," Chili Pop, Chimichurri, Garlic BBQ Sauce, Sweet Chile Marinade, balsamic marinade (see page 82) | For larger fish, you can prevent the need for flipping by keeping the grill closed, or use a grill basket for easier flipping. |

TOTAL TIME: 20 MINUTES PLUS CHILLING / SERVES 16 (MAKES 32 SHOOTERS)

# *yellow tomato* *gazpacho* *shooters*

2 1/2 cups seeded, chopped yellow tomatoes

3 cups chopped yellow seedless watermelon

1 jalapeño pepper, seeded and diced small

1/2 cup small-diced red onion

1/2 cup small-diced yellow bell pepper

2 tablespoons white wine vinegar

2 tablespoons fine extra virgin olive oil

1/4 teaspoon fine grain sea salt

1/2 teaspoon freshly ground black pepper

• In a food processor, blend the tomatoes and watermelon together until smooth, then transfer to a bowl. Stir in the remaining ingredients and add the salt and pepper to taste.

• Store in the refrigerator for at least 2 hours. Stir before serving, then pour into 2-ounce shot glasses; serve cold.

## notes

*If you can't find a yellow watermelon,* any color will do. Just make sure it's unseeded.

*You can make these up to one day in advance,* but if you make them too far in advance, the veggies will lose their crisp. Store covered in the refrigerator.

TOTAL TIME: 1 HOUR / MAKES ABOUT 20 BURGERS

VF

# bean + grain burgers

6 cups water

1/2 teaspoon fine grain sea salt, plus more for cooking water

1 cup dried green lentils

3/4 cup quinoa

6 scallions, chopped

2 large eggs, beaten

1 cup breadcrumbs

2 tablespoons fresh thyme leaves

1/4 teaspoon freshly ground black pepper

Olive oil cooking spray

• In a large pot, bring 4 cups salted water to a boil. Add the lentils and cook over medium heat, uncovered, until tender, about 30 minutes. Drain and cool.

• In a separate pot, add the quinoa and 2 cups water. Cook, covered, over medium heat until the water is absorbed, about 20 minutes. Let cool.

• In a food processor, puree half of the lentils, leaving them somewhat chunky.

• In a large bowl, thoroughly combine the lentils (pureed and whole), quinoa, scallions, eggs, breadcrumbs, thyme, salt, and pepper. Use moistened hands to form the mixture into patties about 2 inches in diameter.

• To grill, cover the cooler side of a grill with aluminum foil and grill the patties for 4 minutes on each side. To cook on a stovetop, spray a skillet with cooking spray and heat over medium heat. Add the patties to the pan, being careful not to let them touch each other. Cook on each side until the sides are browned and the centers are somewhat firm, about 5 minutes.

## notes

*For vegan burgers,* use an egg replacer in lieu of the eggs.

*These are so good* with Cherry Tomato Chutney (page 239), you'll want them for lunch every day.

*Serve with mini buns,* lettuce, and tomato for an American effect, or serve in mini whole-wheat pita pockets with micro greens for a twist.

*Use any type of quinoa* you want for these. The difference will be in the appearance and, subtly, the taste.

# *toppings*

*These are perfect on burgers but also make great toppings for other grilled items, such as shrimp, sausages, and salmon.*

## sautéed **mushrooms**

• Sauté 1/2 pound mixed mushrooms with 1/2 teaspoon salt and 1 tablespoon olive oil for 15 minutes over low heat.

## **mango** relish

• In a food processor, chop 2 peeled, pitted mangoes with 2 scallions, 1/2 cup diced red bell pepper, and 1 tablespoon fresh lime juice until blended but still fairly chunky. Add salt to taste.

## caramelized **onions**

• Slowly sauté 2 sliced onions with 1 teaspoon chopped thyme leaves and 1/2 teaspoon minced garlic in 1 tablespoon olive oil for 30 minutes over low heat.

TOTAL TIME: 60 MINUTES / MAKES ABOUT 3 CUPS

MA V

# cherry tomato *chutney*

4 pints cherry tomatoes, halved

1/2 teaspoon ground allspice

4 cinnamon sticks

1 teaspoon ground cumin

1 teaspoon ground coriander

2 cups apple cider vinegar

1/2 cup turbinado or raw sugar

1/2 teaspoon fine grain sea salt

1/4 teaspoon red chile pepper flakes

• Mix all of the ingredients together in a nonreactive saucepan and cook, uncovered, over low heat until the tomatoes are soft and the liquid is almost gone, about 45 minutes.

• Serve with the Bean and Grain Burgers (page 236).

## notes

**Can be made** up to one week in advance; store covered in the refrigerator.

TOTAL TIME: 10 MINUTES / MAKES ABOUT 1 1/2 CUPS (ENOUGH TO MARINATE 3 POUNDS OF FOOD)

# *chimichurri* marinade

1 cup roughly chopped fresh
flat-leaf parsley

1/2 cup roughly chopped fresh
cilantro

1 teaspoon grated fresh ginger

1/2 clove garlic

1/4 teaspoon ground cumin

1/4 teaspoon ground cinnamon

1 serrano chile pepper

1 teaspoon turbinado or raw
sugar

1/4 cup extra virgin olive oil

2 tablespoons fresh lime juice
(from about 2 limes)

1/2 teaspoon fine grain
sea salt

1/4 teaspoon freshly
ground pepper

• Pulse all ingredients in a
food processor until almost
smooth. Serve over grilled
meats or vegetables. Works
great as a marinade, too!

## notes

**Lobsters or shrimp** are great with this
chimichurri!

**You could also use this as a sauce
for pizza** topped with sautéed or grilled
mushrooms. Put the whole pizza on the
grill for an amazing dish.

**The sauce can be made** one day in
advance; store covered in the
refrigerator.

TOTAL TIME: 60 MINUTES / MAKES ABOUT 1 PINT (ENOUGH TO MARINATE ABOUT 4 POUNDS OF FOOD)

# garlic BBQ sauce

1 tablespoon extra virgin olive oil

1 onion, diced

1/4 cup chopped garlic

2 cups diced tomatoes

1/4 cup molasses

1/4 cup ketchup

1/2 cup turbinado or raw sugar

3 tablespoons fresh thyme leaves

1/2 cup apple cider vinegar

2 tablespoons Dijon mustard

2 bay leaves

• Place a saucepan over medium heat. Add the olive oil and sauté the onion and garlic until translucent, about 3 minutes. Add the remaining ingredients and simmer for 15 minutes.

• Remove the bay leaves and carefully puree everything else in a blender.

• Add the sauce back to the pan and cook for 25 minutes longer over low heat.

## notes

*The amount of food you can cover* will vary depending on how thick you like to lay on the sauce. Remember to leave some untouched by raw meat so guests can slather on more post-grilling if they like.

*Make this sauce in advance;* it will keep in the fridge for up to one week.

TOTAL TIME: 10 MINUTES / MAKES 1 1/2 CUPS (ENOUGH TO MARINATE ABOUT 4 POUNDS OF FOOD)

# *sweet chile marinade*

1/2 cup turbinado or raw sugar

1/2 cup apple cider vinegar

2 tablespoons extra virgin olive oil

1/2 cup chopped shallots

10 cloves garlic, minced

1 tablespoon red chile pepper flakes

1 bay leaf

1 tablespoon Chinese five-spice powder

1/2 teaspoon fine grain sea salt

• Mix everything together in a bowl. Pour the marinade over whatever you are grilling and cover the item with plastic wrap.

• For meats, turn the item every hour or so for at least 4 hours but not longer than overnight. For tofu and fish, marinate for 1 hour. Veggies can be grilled right away.

## *notes*

*Give yourself plenty of time* if you are marinating meats with this recipe.

*Marinade can be made* one or two days in advance; store covered in the refrigerator.

# spice mixes

*Simply combine the ingredients for your preferred spice mix together in a bowl. Add 1 1/2 tablespoons of spice per pound of your desired grill item before grilling.*

TOTAL TIME: 5 MINUTES

# "the colonel"

2 teaspoons garlic powder

2 teaspoons onion powder

2 teaspoons dried thyme

2 teaspoons dried oregano

1 teaspoon mustard powder

1/2 teaspoon freshly ground black pepper

1 teaspoon cayenne pepper

1 teaspoon fine grain sea salt

## notes

*This spice mix can be made in advance* and stored in your pantry for weeks.

*"The Colonel"* is named after the spice man from whom we got all of our spices while recipe testing in Cincinnati, Ohio—The Colonel of Spices.

TOTAL TIME: 5 MINUTES

S MA V

# *chili pop*

1/2 teaspoon cayenne pepper

1/4 cup chili powder

1/2 teaspoon freshly ground black pepper

1 teaspoon paprika

1 teaspoon fine grain sea salt

*notes*

*This spice mix can be made in advance* and stored in your pantry for weeks.

TOTAL TIME: 5 MINUTES

S MA V

# *lime of my life*

1 tablespoon grated lime zest, loosely packed

1/4 cup fresh lime juice (from about 4 limes)

1 tablespoon extra virgin olive oil

1 tablespoon garam masala

1 teaspoon ground cumin

1 1/2 teaspoons fine grain sea salt

*notes*

*You can mix the dried spices in advance,* but add the lime zest, juice, and olive oil just before use.

TOTAL TIME: 50 MINUTES / SERVES 8

# chickpea peppadew *salad*

2 eggplants, cut into 1-inch cubes

1 tablespoon extra virgin olive oil

1/4 cup balsamic vinegar

4 tablespoons fine extra virgin olive oil

1 shallot, chopped

1 clove garlic, chopped

2 tablespoons fresh lemon juice (from about 1 lemon)

2 teaspoons grated lemon zest

1/2 teaspoon fine grain sea salt

1/4 teaspoon freshly ground black pepper

10 Peppadew peppers, seeded and quartered

1 1/2 cups cooked chickpeas

1 cup cubed feta cheese

1/4 cup chopped fresh mint leaves

• Preheat the oven to 400°F. Toss the eggplant with 1 tablespoon olive oil and spread out on a rimmed baking sheet. Roast for 30 minutes, stirring halfway through. Let cool.

• MAKE THE VINAIGRETTE: Whisk together the vinegar, fine olive oil, shallot, garlic, lemon juice and zest, salt, and pepper until thoroughly combined.

• In a large bowl, toss the cooled eggplant with the vinaigrette. Add the peppers, chickpeas, feta, and mint. Toss again. Serve cold or at room temperature.

## notes

**Peppadew peppers** often come pickled in jars. They are mild or hot, red or yellow; all work in this recipe, although we prefer hot reds. Use roasted red peppers if Peppadews aren't available to you.

**For tips on cooking chickpeas,** see Quick Reference (page 257).

**This can be made** one day in advance; store covered in the refrigerator.

TOTAL TIME: 25 MINUTES / SERVES 10

MA V

# grilled corn *with avocado crema*

10 ears corn

2 ripe Hass avocados, pitted and peeled

Juice and zest of 2 limes

1/4 cup extra virgin olive oil

1/4 teaspoon fine grain sea salt

1/4 teaspoon cayenne pepper

• Preheat a grill to medium heat. Shuck the corn and grill for 15 minutes, turning it so that all sides are cooked evenly. Alternatively, boil the shucked corn for 10 minutes.

• Add the remaining ingredients to a blender and puree until smooth. Spread avocado crema on each piece of corn to serve.

## notes

**The dressing can be made** one day in advance; store covered in the refrigerator.

**This avocado dressing** is great to use the next day on a plain, toasted tortilla or quick cheese quesadilla for lunch.

TOTAL TIME: 45 MINUTES / SERVES 12

MA V

# *fingerling potato salad*
## *with celery leaves*

3 pounds fingerling potatoes

1/2 teaspoon fine grain sea salt, plus more for water

2 tablespoons grainy mustard

1/3 cup white wine vinegar

1/3 cup fine extra virgin olive oil

1/4 teaspoon freshly ground black pepper

4 cups baby arugula

1 cup celery leaves

• Slice the potatoes into 1/2-inch chunks. Place them in a pot of salted water over high heat. Boil the potatoes until a knife inserts easily but with a bit of resistance, 10 to 12 minutes. Drain and let sit for 5 minutes.

• Combine the mustard, vinegar, olive oil, 1/2 teaspoon salt, and pepper together in a bowl. Add the potatoes while still warm and stir. Let cool, then refrigerate until ready to serve. At service, stir in the arugula and celery leaves.

*notes*

*You can cook and dress the potatoes* one day in advance, but add the celery and arugula closer to serving time so they do not wilt. Store the dressed potatoes covered in the refrigerator.

TOTAL TIME: 15 MINUTES / SERVES 8

S V

# *grilled grapefruit*

*1 pink grapefruit*

*1 yellow grapefruit*

*4 teaspoons turbinado or raw sugar*

• Preheat grill to medium-high heat. Slice each grapefruit into 8 wedges and line them up peel side down on a platter. Rub each side of flesh with 1/4 teaspoon (or less) of sugar.

• Grill the slices flesh side down for 3 minutes. Turn the slices once to grill the other side of the flesh for an additional 3 minutes. The grapefruit will be bursting with warm juice and the sugar will caramelize on the surface.

## *notes*

***Josie makes*** a version of this in her broiler when grilling season is over.

TOTAL TIME: 10 MINUTES PLUS CHILLING / SERVES 6 TO 8

MA V

# *pucker punch*

*1/2 pound green grapes*

*1 orange*

*2 white peaches, pitted*

*1 bottle white wine*

*1 1/2 cups Lillet blanc*

• Slice the grapes in halves or quarters. Slice the orange into rounds and then quarters, keeping the peel on, and chop the peaches into 1-inch chunks.

• In a jug, carafe, or pitcher mix the fruit with the wine and Lillet. Let chill for 2 hours and up to overnight before serving.

• Serve cold. Welcome your guests to nibble on the fruit as they sip their drinks.

*notes*

*This drink gets better* after it sits for a few hours and the fruit really has a chance to soak in all the liquid. Try to make it a few hours or up to one day in advance. Store covered in the refrigerator.

# BUILD YOUR OWN BASH

## APPETIZERS

- Arugula + Mozzarella Salad w. Eggplant Caponata...*58*
- Asparagus w. Poached Egg + Panko...*129*
- Avocado Toasts...*70*
- Beets w. Citrus + Ginger Goat Cheese...*165*
- Caramelized Onion Crème Fraîche w. Blistered Veggies...*86*
- Cheese Plate w. Spiced Kumquat Jam...*210*
- Chicken + Apricot Falafel...*212*
- Chile Lime Almonds...*50*
- Chorizo Red Pepper Polenta Squares...*220*
- Crab Fritters w. Creamy Mustard Sauce...*65*
- Edamame Dumplings...*108*
- Fava Bean Pesto Bruschetta...*35*
- Fennel Salad w. Grapefruit Vinaigrette...*159*
- The Granola Mash-Up...*148*
- Green Salad w. Basil Balsamic Dressing...*199*
- Herbed Goat Cheese Toasts w. Salmon Roe...*215*
- Herbed Heirloom Tomato Salad...*51*
- Iceberg Wedges w. Honey Corn Vinaigrette...*135*
- Kimchi Scallion Pancakes...*43*
- Roasted Garlic...*75*
- Rosemary + Olive Oil Popcorn...*187*
- Shrimp Cocktail...*216*
- Slow-Baked Red Bell Peppers...*29*
- Spiced Roasted Chickpeas...*81*
- Spicy Lemon + Date Chutney w. Warm Pita...*214*
- Spinach + Cremini Split Pea Soup...*171*
- Sweet Pea + Zucchini Cakes...*217*
- Sweet Pea Guacamole...*100*
- Tatsoi Salad w. Carrot Ginger Dressing...*113*
- Tomato Tartlets...*193*
- Tuna Poke...*219*
- Watercress + Pear Salad w. Date Vinaigrette...*116*
- Watermelon Black Pepper Salad...*92*
- Yellow Tomato Gazpacho Shooters...*235*

## ENTREES

- Baked Eggs over Spinach...*149*
- Balsamic-Marinated Salmon...*82*
- Bean + Grain Burgers...*236*
- Black-Eyed Peas...*66*
- Braised Short Ribs w. Pomegranate Onions...*117*
- Butternut Squash + Spinach Lasagna...*36*
- Challah French Toast w. Honeyed Ricotta + Blueberry Vanilla Jam...*150*
- Cheese + Tofu Quesadillas...*71*
- Collard-Wrapped Burritos...*102*
- Filet Mignon w. Wedding Sauce...*161*
- Fried Chicken w. Gravy...*136*
- Granola-Crusted Cod...*94*
- Kale + Ricotta Ravioli...*176*
- Mediterranean Roasted Pork Loin...*60*
- Miso Caper Glazed Salmon...*87*
- Oyster Mushroom + Sage Orzo...*173*
- Pepita-Crusted Tofu...*46*
- Potato Kalamata Pizza...*189*
- Red Miso BBQ Pork w. Pineapple Jam...*44*
- Roasted Vegetable Enchiladas...*52*
- Scallops w. Blood Orange Citronette...*130*
- Sea Bass w. Tomato + Olive Gremolata...*200*
- Seafood Cobb...*143*
- Seafood Stew...*166*
- Seared Tofu + Couscous Salad...*194*
- Shrimp, Bok Choy + Eggplant Stir Fry...*111*
- Skirt Steak w. Quick Pickled Leeks, Scapes + Gigante Beans...*76*
- Spicy Saffron Shrimp w. Yellow Peppers...*188*
- Whole Roasted Fish Stuffed w. Herbs...*31*

-------- [ MAKE YOUR OWN COURSE SELECTIONS FOR AN EVENT PERFECTLY TAILORED TO YOU! ] --------

**SIDES**

- Cayenne-Flecked Corn Pudding...*83*
- Chickpea Peppadew Salad...*246*
- Chile Garlic Broccolini...*39*
- Chipotle Sweet Potato Salad...*72*
- Cider-Braised Collards...*66*
- Coconut Rice...*112*
- Corn + Tomato Salad...*101*
- Creamy Basil Polenta w. Buttons + Shiitakes...*32*
- Cumin-Spiced Carrots...*195*
- Fingerling Potato Salad w. Celery Leaves...*249*
- Green Goddess Purple Potatoes...*144*
- Grilled Corn w. Avocado Crema...*248*
- Herbed Heirloom Tomato Salad...*51*
- Mango Chile Cabbage Slaw...*47*
- Minted Wheatberry Salad w. Peas...*127*
- Onion Tart w. Gruyère Crust...*152*
- Orrechiette + Green Bean Salad...*95*
- Roasted Cauliflower Salad...*118*
- Roasted Sweet Potatoes w. Pistachios...*61*
- Rosemary Lentils w. Walnuts...*180*
- Sharp Cheddar + Chive Waffles...*139*
- Slow Baked Red Bell Peppers...*29*
- Smoky Kale + Chickpeas...*78*
- Truffle-Laced Potatoes w. Artichoke Hearts + Leeks...*162*
- Warm Quinoa, Kale + Goat Cheese Salad...*201*
- Warm Squash Salad w. Farro, Hazelnuts + Currants...*89*

**DESSERTS**

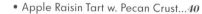

- Almond Cookies w. Cherries + Cream...*62*
- Apple Raisin Tart w. Pecan Crust...*40*
- Apricot Shortcakes w. Five Spice Whipped Cream...*167*
- Baked Peaches w. Gingersnap Crumble...*68*
- Black Sesame Brittle...*114*
- Cherry Watermelon Granita...*84*
- Chocolate Black Pepper Cakes...*190*
- Chocolate Chip Cookies...*223*
- Cinnamon Corn Ice Cream w. Blueberries...*96*
- Coconut Rhubarb Crumble w. Raspberry Whipped Cream...*133*
- Crispy Chocolate Banana Bread Pudding...*163*
- Espresso Cinnamon Crisps...*120*
- Fig Truffles...*196*
- Green Chile-Glazed Pineapple...*73*
- Grilled Grapefruit...*250*
- Hazelnut Budino...*174*
- Horchata Pops...*56*
- Lavender Shortbread Cookies...*222*
- Lychee, Honeydew + Mint Sorbet...*48*
- Maple Cream Cheese Cookie Sandwiches...*90*
- Mexican Goddess Chocolate Pudding...*106*
- Red Wine + Blueberry Sorbet...*181*
- Semolina + Orange Cake...*33*
- Snowed-In Berries...*202*
- Spiced Stone Fruit Salad...*146*
- Strawberry Cornmeal Cake...*79*

**DRINKS**

- The Cortez...*121*
- Dream Sequins...*98*
- Grapefruit Blackberry Flirt...*225*
- Hibiscus Iced Tea...*140*
- Pucker Punch...*251*
- Twinkle Toes...*225*

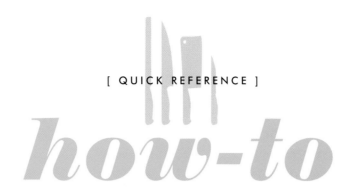

# how-to

## *blanch*

------------------------------------------------

This procedure cooks a vegetable while retaining its color and crunchy texture. Submerge the cleaned and trimmed vegetable in a large pot of boiling water for a minute or two. Quickly remove it with tongs or drain the pot and submerge the vegetables in a large bowl of cold water with ice cubes, or run it under very cold water. Don't let the vegetable sit too long, just until cooled.

## *butterfly meat*

------------------------------------------------

Butterflying meat is usually done with a thick, boneless piece of meat that needs to be flattened out. In this book, we've butterflied meat into thirds so we can stuff it, covering as much surface area as possible with flavor, and then rolling or folding it back up. For smaller cuts of meat, simply butterfly in half, slicing the meat so that it opens like a book.

To butterfly in thirds, place the meat on a cutting board so that the grain runs up and down. Place one hand on the meat to hold it in place. With a large, sharp knife in the other hand, begin cutting the meat about 2/3 of the way down, parallel to the cutting board, starting at one side and stopping before it's cut all the way through. Open the meat like a book where the knife stopped; this is the first hinge.

With the piece of meat lying flat on the cutting board, the grain still running up and down, begin cutting the thicker side of the meat. Starting at the hinge and cutting in the same direction, cut the thicker side in half. Stop before reaching the other side. This is the second hinge. Open the piece of meat completely. The resulting piece of meat should be three times wider and three times thinner than the original piece.

## *char*

To char, heat a pan with a little oil. Add the ingredient you wish to char and leave it alone until it has blackened (it's tempting to move the ingredient around, but don't). After it blackens, i.e., becomes charred, move the ingredient around so that it does not stick to the bottom of the pan. You can also char food on a grill.

## *chiffonade*

Place the leaves of leafy vegetables or herbs on top of each other, roll them up, and slice thinly. Unroll the leaves for long, thin strips.

## *cook dried beans*

-------------------------------------------------------------------

Dried beans can take hours to cook, so plan ahead. Use this method to cook any type of legume, including chickpeas and black-eyed peas. Lentils, split peas, and fresh shell beans don't require soaking, and they cook more quickly.

**RINSE:**

Rinse your beans to rid them of dirt or sand before soaking.

**SOAK:**

Beans should soak in water, uncovered, in the refrigerator overnight. Strain the beans and use fresh water to cook. Alternatively, add the beans to a large pot of water. Bring the water to a boil for two minutes. Turn off the water and let the beans sit for 1 hour. Proceed to cooking instructions.

**AVOID MUSHY BEANS:**

Do not add salt to your beans during the cooking step. This may cause the beans to burst open and get mushy and have a mealy texture. Additionally, don't boil your beans very hard. Keep them at a medium simmer.

**COOK:**

After soaking, add the beans to a large pot of clean water; the water should cover the beans by at least four inches. Add a bay leaf, a garlic clove, and a few black peppercorns to the water. (We don't directly call for this step in our recipes, but if you want to add them, they'll add an extra depth of flavor that will wow your guests.) Simmer for two to three hours, stirring occasionally. Add more water if necessary to maintain at least two inches of cooking liquid above the beans. The beans are done when they are fork-tender. The inside should be like a thick, creamy, mashed potato, not granular or mealy. Different beans have different cooking times: test the beans from time to time for doneness. Once they are done, drain off the cooking liquid immediately or the beans will continue to cook.

*continued*

**USE:**

Generally, when a recipe calls for beans, it assumes beans drained of liquid. However, to store any unused beans, keep them in the cooking liquid.

To save time on party day, cook beans ahead of time and freeze them in a sealed plastic container. Use some of the cooking liquid to cover the beans in the container to avoid freezer burn. If you simply don't have the time or just forgot to cook your beans, a no- or low-sodium canned variety will work with all of our dishes that call for beans. Just rinse the beans thoroughly.

## *cut corn off the cob*

To cut corn from the cob, first shuck the corn. Lay the corn on a cutting board and slice the kernels off. Now it'll be easy to flip the corn onto the flat, just-sliced side, and slice the next side. Repeat until all sides have been cut and the cob is totally bare.

## *deglaze a pan*

Often when you are searing or roasting, there are brown residual bits of food on the pan after you remove the main item. That caramelized residue can add extra flavor to your dish in the form of a sauce. Deglazing a pan removes that residue from the bottom of the pan and incorporates it into the sauce. Here's how:

If there is a lot of fat or oil in the pan, pour that fat into another container or discard. With the pan over medium heat, add a bit of liquid; use whatever is called for in the recipe (usually wine, stock, or vinegar). With a spoon or spatula scrape up the brown bits. The pan is now deglazed; continue with your recipe.

## *hard-boil eggs*

Add eggs to a pot that's large enough for the eggs to be covered by three inches of water. Add one teaspoon white vinegar. Bring the water to a boil and then turn off the heat immediately. Cover the pot and let the eggs sit in the water for 10 minutes. Transfer them to a bowl of cold water until cool. An interesting fact: older eggs (those closer to their expiration date) will peel more easily than newer eggs.

## *peel hazelnuts*
--------------------------------------------------------------

To peel hazelnuts, roast the shelled nuts in the oven for about five minutes. Transfer them to a sealed, heatproof container while they are still hot for five to ten minutes. Using a clean, dry towel, rub the skins off of the nuts one handful at a time.

Just a heads up: there will always be a few nuts that are hard to peel or don't peel at all. You can just set them aside, nibble on them yourself, and continue the recipe.

## *poach eggs*
--------------------------------------------------------------

Poaching eggs can seem overly complicated and daunting. Chefs have all kinds of tricks to try to keep the egg whites in a round shape—the whites tend to spread all over the place and look messy. When you're poaching several eggs, many of these tricks can quickly become annoying and stressful.

There are a few things that we do to keep egg poaching practically effortless. Use a wide pan that is about three inches in height. Fill it halfway with water and bring it to a light simmer.

Crack an egg into a cup, hold the cup right over the water, and gently tilt the cup letting the egg slip into the simmering water. When you start to see the whites set up, repeat with another egg. Be sure to leave about an inch of space between the eggs. Remove the eggs with a slotted spoon after four or five minutes of cooking.

Don't be alarmed to see some whites stretch out from the egg. Once the egg is done cooking you can just tear them off.

## *slice leeks*

-------------------------------------------------------------

Cut leeks by trimming the root and using only the lower white part
and palest green part. Slice rings and wash well. Discard the
rest of the stalk or use it for a homemade stock.

## *suprême*

-------------------------------------------------------------

Suprême is a fancy way to describe a segment or wedge of citrus fruit
with the skin, pith, membranes, and seeds removed. This can be done
with citrus fruit like oranges, grapefruits, pomelo, lemons, and limes.

Cut off the ends of your fruit and stand the fruit on one of the ends.
Following the shape of the fruit, cut away the skin and white pith,
revealing the flesh. Over a bowl, slice into the flesh of the fruit on both
sides of each membrane to remove the segments. The bowl will catch
the juice. Remove any seeds.

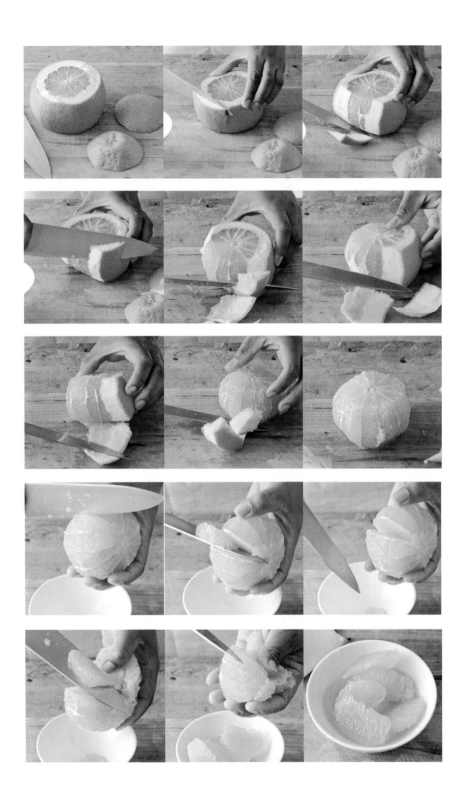

## test oil temperature

If you don't have a deep-fry thermometer on hand, try this: drop a 1-inch piece of torn bread into the oil when you think it may be ready. If it takes about a minute to brown, the oil is ready. If it browns in 10 seconds, then it's probably too hot and you should lower or turn off the heat for a little while.

## toast nuts

**PAN TOASTING:**

For one cup of nuts, add one teaspoon of oil to a frying pan. Heat the oil over medium heat. Add the nuts, stirring occasionally until the nuts are golden and fragrant, three to five minutes. You can also toast nuts "dry," i.e., without oil. Keep a watchful eye on them—it's the worst when you burn them!

**OVEN TOASTING:**

Spread the nuts evenly on a rimmed baking sheet. Bake them in a 350°F to 375°F oven for about ten minutes. Stir halfway through for even toasting.

Smaller nuts, like pine nuts or sliced almonds, cook faster and burn quickly. A good hint: if you smell them, take them out right away. They will continue to brown if left on the hot baking sheet outside of the oven.

## toast/grill bread

Heat a grill or broiler to medium heat. Slice the bread to desired size. Lay the bread on a cookie sheet. Brush one side of the bread with olive oil or melted butter, or simply use olive oil cooking spray. To broil, place the cookie sheet in the broiler with the brushed side of the bread facing the heat. Broil until toasty and browned. Broilers can be hard to control so watch the bread closely. If you only need to toast a small amount of bread, a regular toaster oven will do the job. To grill, place the bread directly on the grill, oil side down. Wait 2 to 3 minutes, until grill lines appear, and remove from the grill.

### truss meat

----------------------------------------

Trussing is a way of tying up a piece of meat with string so that it's more compact. The goal of trussing is to create a neat appearance and a more uniform thickness so that the meat cooks evenly. How to truss depends on the type of meat or cut you have. Use butcher's twine or silicone rubber bands sold for this purpose. With boneless roasts, you can tie off the string 1 inch apart. If any part of the roast is much thinner than the rest, go ahead and double it over before tying. For poultry, tuck the wing tips behind the bird and tie the legs closed.

### use a vanilla bean

----------------------------------------

Slice the bean lengthwise in half. Lay flat with the interior facing up. Using your knife, throroughly scrape the tiny black seeds from the inside of the pod onto your knife and add them to whatever you are making. You can put the pods into your dish while it cooks as well; just remember to remove them before serving.

### whip cream

----------------------------------------

"Cream," "heavy cream," "heavy whipping cream," "light whipping cream," and "whipping cream" are all used to make whipped cream. Pick a cream that has at least 30 percent fat. For a faster whip, be sure that your whisk, bowl, and cream are cold. Try putting all of these in the fridge or freezer for fifteen minutes. And always make sure your bowl and whisk are clean.

You can add a bit of sugar, extract (vanilla, almond, etc.), spice (cinnamon, nutmeg, garam masala), liqueur (Grand Marnier, amaretto), or fruit puree to flavor your cream.

You can whip the cream to soft-medium peaks or nice firm peaks. If you whip it too far past a firm peak, your whipped cream will most likely be too firm to serve, and you should start over with new cream. If you really go crazy with the whipping, your cream will turn to butter.

# sources

## INGREDIENTS

**Coconut Oil:** Specializing in quality coconut-based products, visit this site for the skinny on coconut oil.
tropicaltraditions.com

**Edible Gold Dust:** Use this in our Twinkle Toes cocktail (page 225).
anoccasionalchocolate.com

**Hibiscus Flowers:** Hibiscus may also be called "dried sorrel."
serendipitea.com

**Kumquats:** Our kumquat jam (page 241) is well worth the extra effort to score this fruit!
kumquatgrowers.com

**Local Farmers' Market or Farm-Share:** Use this lengthy (though not totally complete) directory to find quality, farm-fresh ingredients near you.
localharvest.org

**Miscellaneous Ingredients:** Zingerman's is excellent for baked goods, cheese, oils, and vinegars. Cube Marketplace is another great source for imported oils, vinegars, and special pastas.
zingermans.com, cubemarketplace.com

**Spices, Vanilla Beans, Lavender:** HerbsSpice is the online component of The Colonel Spice Man from Jill's hometown in Cincinnati, Ohio. The other two sites are world-renown sources for spices of all kinds.
herbsspice.com, kalustyans.com, penzeys.com

**Vegan Egg Replacer:** Order online or look for egg replacer in health food stores.
ener-g.com

**Whole Grains + Flours**: Order online or look for products in health food and grocery stores near you.
bobsredmill.com

**Wine + Spirits:** Union Square Wines has the best selection and they deliver!
unionsquarewines.com

## EQUIPMENT

**Japanese Mandoline:** Josie and Jill swear by this one.
http://store.bowerykitchens.com/benmanslic.html

**Kitchen Tools:** Good sources for sometimes hard to find equipment and tools. Broadway Panhandler and Bowery Kitchen also have physical locations in NYC.
bakedeco.com, wilton.com, broadwaypanhandler.com, bowerykitchens.com

## WEB SITES

**Seafood Watch:** A great resource for tracking endangered seafood species.
montereybayaquarium.org

**USDA:** Use this site to understand agricultural marketing and why your food is labeled organic or otherwise.
ams.usda.gov

## FILMS

• **Food, Inc.,** directed by Robert Kenner. A documentary that illuminates the state of the American food industry.

• **The Future of Food**, directed by Deborah Koons Garcia. A documentary exposing companies that rely too heavily on the bottom line as their driving factor rather than providing the world with healthy food.

## BOOKS + MAGAZINES

• **The Art of Eating** by Edward Behr A quarterly magazine devoted to analyzing food origins and specific topics in food.

• **Eating Animals** by Jonathon Safran Foer. Investigative-style writing that delves deep into the United States large-scale factory farms. The author interviews numerous insiders to get all sides of the story.

• **Food Rules: An Eater's Manual** by Michael Pollan. A quick, witty guide to what to eat and what not to eat.

• **The Kitchen Diaries** by Nigel Slater. A cookbook that effortlessly walks readers through a year of seasonal eating.

• **Martha Stewart's Cooking School** by Martha Stewart. An excellent how-to book for beginner chefs that teaches technique through simple recipes.

# index